DESPERATELY SEEKING HARING

IAN CASTELLO-CORTES

GINGKO PRESS

A VERY SQUARE CHILDHOOD

Keith's childhood could not have been more straightforward. He came from a loving home, a dad with a stable job, a stay-at-home mom, and with three younger sisters. All the children had names beginning with 'K' – suggesting a degree of wholesome humour from his parents – Keith, Kay, Karen and Kristen. He attended the local school, did a paper round, became very bored with small town life, got into the Jesus movement and then had a teenage rebellion taking drugs and really getting into the Grateful Dead. He had his share of girlfriends and lost his virginity to a girl named Suzy, his first serious early relationship, with whom he went hitch-hiking. They had lots of sex. There was no hint at this point that he would become very openly gay. He decided to go to art school because he liked drawing and thought commercial art could offer a career – nothing more intense than that. He picked Pittsburgh because it seemed to make sense. Little did he know that Pittsburgh would change his life.

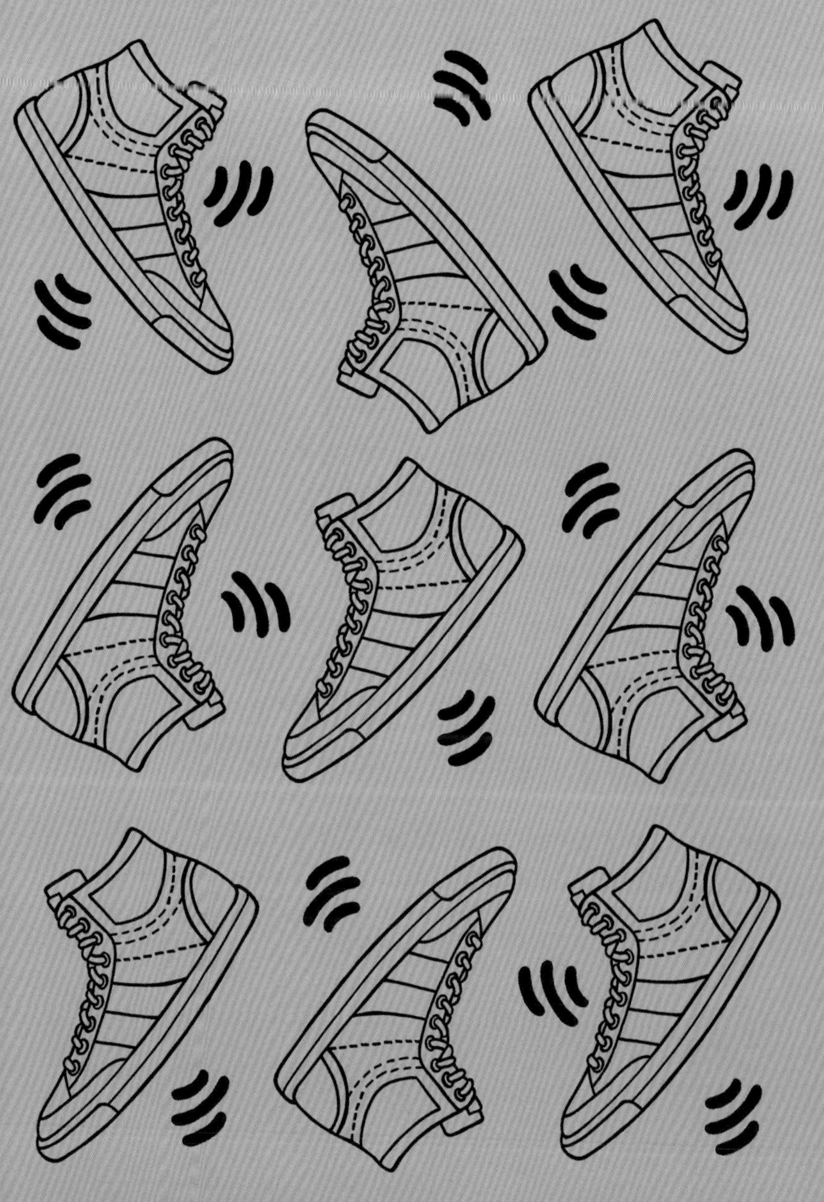

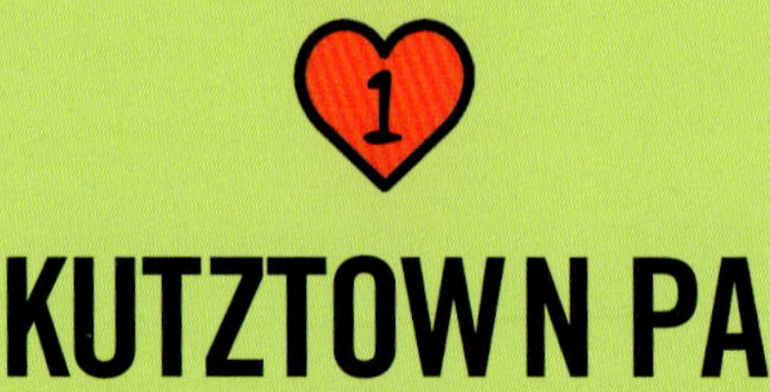

KUTZTOWN PA

"Allen was a church-going, Nixon-supporting Republican."
The Guardian, on Keith's dad.

Keith's was the most ordinary, straightforward all-American childhood. His dad, Allen, and mum, Joan had met in high school in Kutztown, and returned there to raise their family. From being in the Marines, Allen took a safe job-for-life at AT&T. Joan thought of becoming a teacher, but then decided to be a housewife and mother. But you can never really tell where the spark that lights the next artworld success comes from. In later life Keith put it down to the fact that Allan was a really good amateur cartoonist, and showed the young Keith how to do them from a very young age. It was perhaps this naïve, instant cartoon line-driven style which became Keith's automatic visual language, an aesthetic that later struck an instantly appreciated chord in Europe, Japan and the USA.

WHERE?
HIGH STREET, KUTZTOWN, PA.

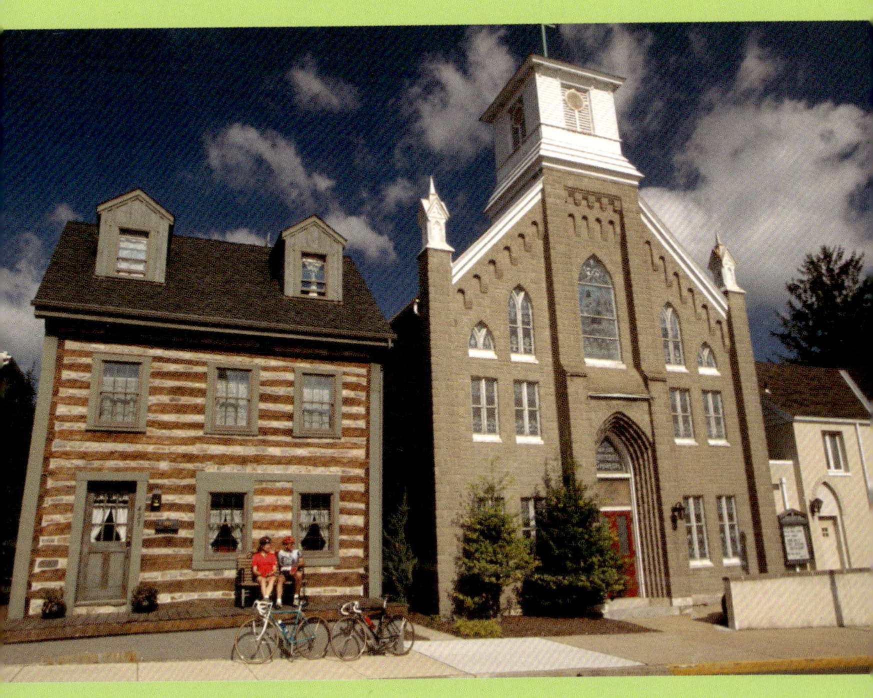

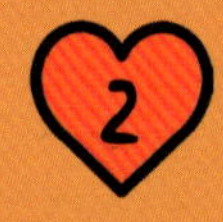

JESUS SAVES

"In his early teens he was, for a time, a Jesus freak." Rolling Stone

With the white-bread US family – clean-living, simple, decent – came the usual conventional religious sensibility. But into this neat suburban world came an external influence that grabbed Keith's attention when he was only 12: a Hare Krishna group. To Keith they seemed wonderfully exotic, with their saffron robes and chants and incantations. He loved their "Jesus Saves" leaflets. Allen and Joan noticed that some of these Jesus graphics started finding their way into Keith's drawings. At this point it was just instictive – a quality that Keith managed to maintain for the rest of his life. Something very clever in his makeup made him realise that replicating that innocent, instant and almost child-like response was what would make his art so new, so attractive.

WHAT?
'JESUS SAVES' SIGNAGE, KUTZTOWN, PA.

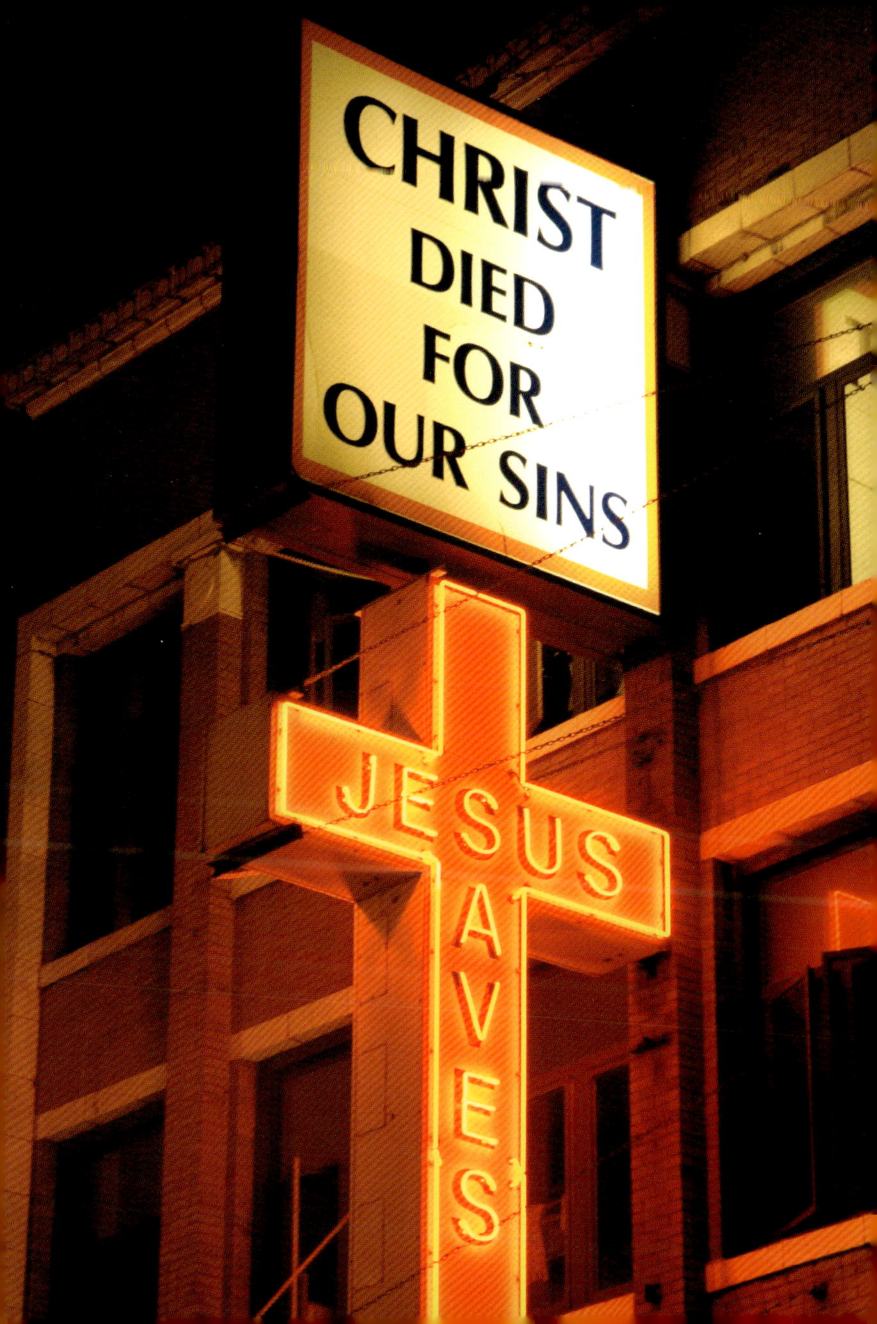
CHRIST
DIED
FOR
OUR SINS
JESUS
SAVES

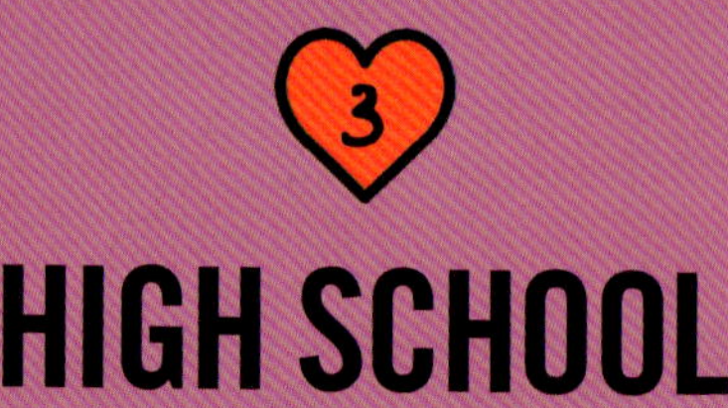

HIGH SCHOOL

"Drugs showed me a whole new world."
Keith Haring in Rolling Stone

Keith was curious, open to new ideas and loved experimenting. He also became conscious of the tedious conformity of Kutztown. It was at high school that he discovered the Grateful Dead, got into a new set of 'trouble-makers' and started dropping acid and, worse, angel dust. Gerry Garcia's world was infinitely more interesting than the prospect of a suburban existence, so much more intriguing than the drone of lessons at school. To identify with his new discovery, in standard teenage fashion, Keith grew his hair long. Almost anticipating his meeting with Timothy Leary many years later, Keith became fascinated at how drugs altered his perceptions. There was a degree of alienation from his family, but it was a price that needed to be paid.

WHO?
THE GRATEFUL DEAD IN 1974.
THE CULT FOLLOWERS OF THE DRUGGY BAND WERE KNOWN AS 'DEADHEADS'. KEITH WAS PROUD TO CALL HIMSELF ONE DURING HIS TEENAGE YEARS.

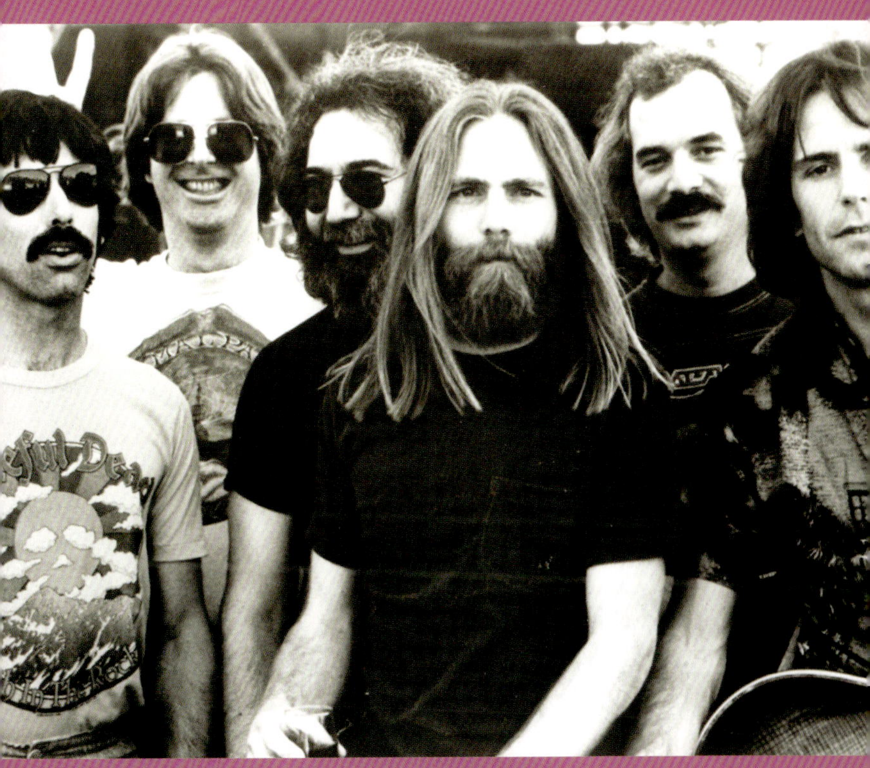

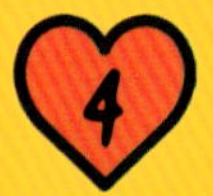

LONG BEACH ISLAND, NJ

***"Every age is an age of anxiety...for us it was knowing that, at any moment, our world could blow up."* Carlo McCormick, curator and critic, in The Guardian.**

Against his parents' wishes, in 1975, aged 17, Keith left home in the middle of the night, to go and work in Ocean City. He lodged in a boarding house where he first came into contact with kids from New York, many of them Jewish. To Keith it felt like contact with a different culture, it was his first time trying to seduce girls and wondering why he wasn't succeeding, and his first, then unrecognised, gay feelings. Keith loved the beach and the nights on acid watching sunrise come up. After the squareness of Kutztown the summer was a kind of catharsis, which allowed him to return home to his parents and led to a more controlled relationship with drugs: from now on it would be mostly pot. Keith also now decided to go to art school.

WHERE?
SUNSET ON OCEAN CITY BEACH, NEW JERSEY.

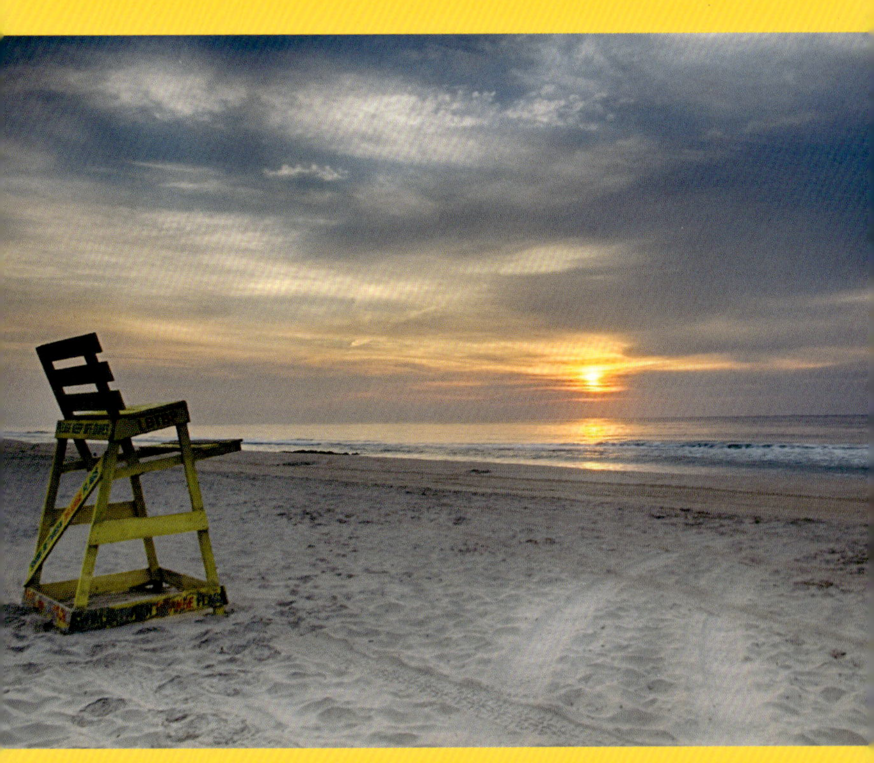

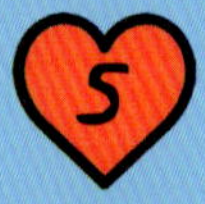

THE IVY ART SCHOOL

"All real works of art look as though they were done in joy." **Robert Henri**

After some discussion, Keith picked the Ivy Art School as the place to go. He enrolled in the graphic design course, which was focused on commercial art. This was Keith being sensible – it would ensure that he could earn a living. At the Ivy School he met his first girlfriend – Suzy. They had a close, very sexual relationship. She and Keith would get turned on by looking at *Penthouse* magazine. It was in the late '70s that the magazine began featuring couples in simulated sex situations and Keith started to realise that perhaps he found the naked guys turned him on more than the girls. For now he kept that knowledge to himself. In parallel he began to be turned off by the commercial art course. Perhaps feeling that he had to be true to his real sexuality, he in parallel felt he should follow his artistic instincts; reading *The Art Spirit*, by US artist Robert Henri, convinced him: he would have to leave the Ivy.

WHAT?
PENTHOUSE MAGAZINE, WHICH IN THE 1970S HAD SOME UNINTENDED HOMO-EROTIC ELEMENTS, HELPED KEITH APPRECIATE HIS TRUE SEXUALITY.

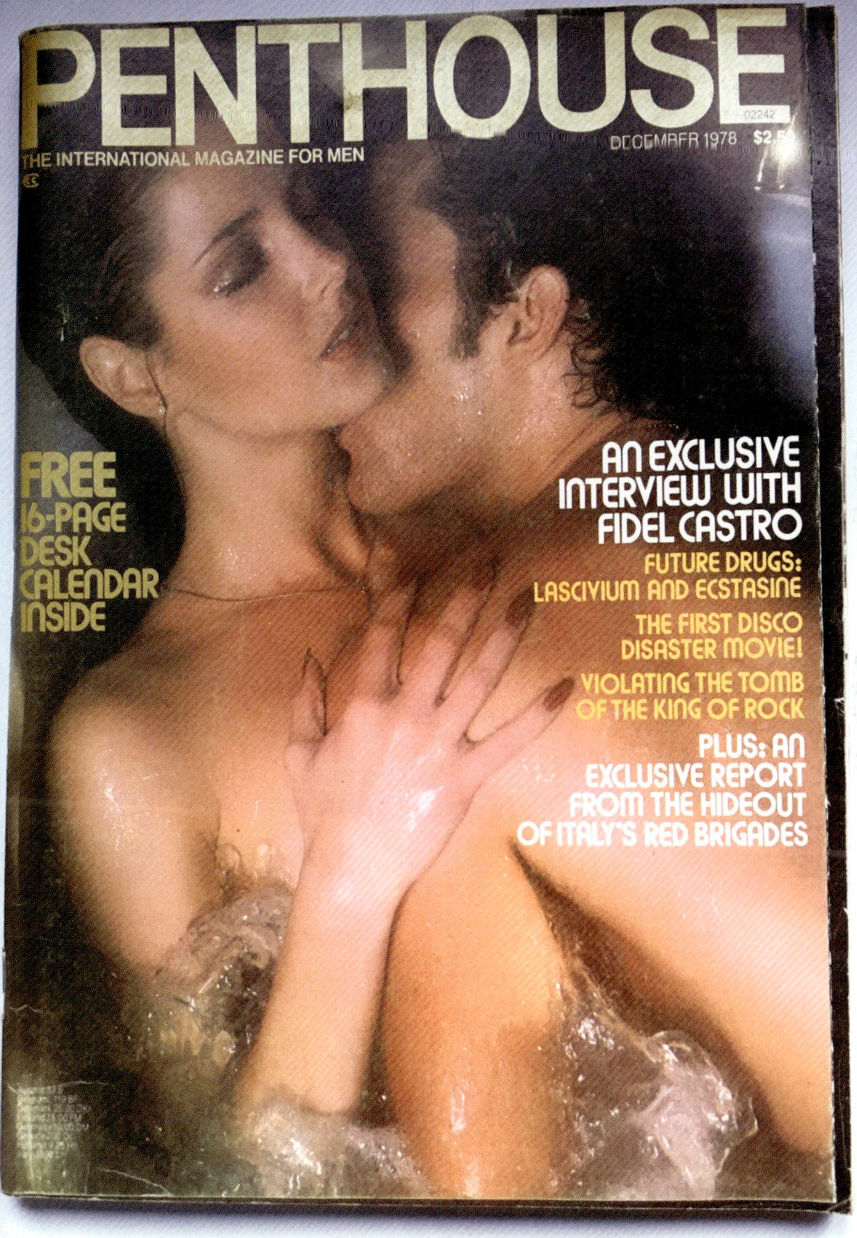

PENTHOUSE

THE INTERNATIONAL MAGAZINE FOR MEN

02242

DECEMBER 1978 $2.5

FREE 16-PAGE DESK CALENDAR INSIDE

AN EXCLUSIVE INTERVIEW WITH FIDEL CASTRO

FUTURE DRUGS: LASCIVIUM AND ECSTASINE

THE FIRST DISCO DISASTER MOVIE!

VIOLATING THE TOMB OF THE KING OF ROCK

PLUS: AN EXCLUSIVE REPORT FROM THE HIDEOUT OF ITALY'S RED BRIGADES

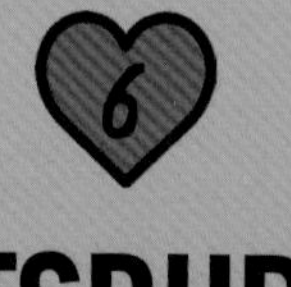

PITTSBURGH

"Pittsburgh...is the workhorse of America's north-east. It is steel, sweat, toil."

The Telegraph

It's amazing how heavy-industrial Pittsburgh was the cradle of both Andy Warhol and Keith Haring. Whilst Warhol had formally enrolled at the upscale Carnegie Institute Keith arrived at the Pittsburgh Center for the Arts, housed in a handsome 17th Century-style mansion, almost as an imposter. He got a job there as a maintenance guy – helping local artists stage their works. In his faux-naïf way, Keith was soon attending print-making classes, sitting in on lectures, reading voraciously in the library and even eating at the college canteen. To all intents and purposes he became a student, without having enrolled. Keith was hyper-open to any new experiences – not just art, but people, not least the young black workers at the Center for the Arts. This is when Keith's affinity for black culture first developed.

WHERE?
PITTSBURGH, WITH RUSTING INDUSTRIAL PLANT, LOOKING ACROSS TOWARDS THE SLEEKER DOWNTOWN.

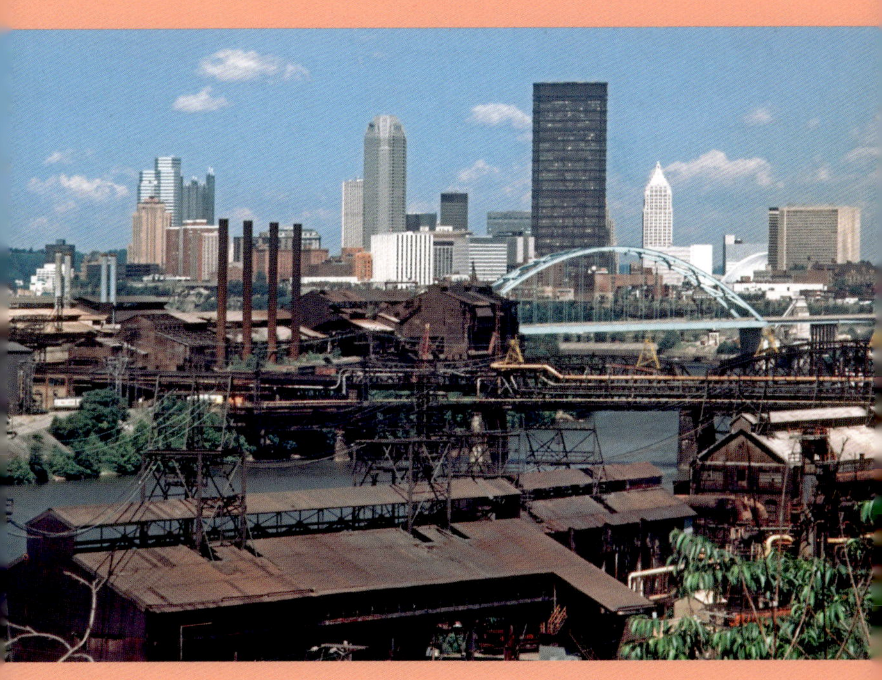

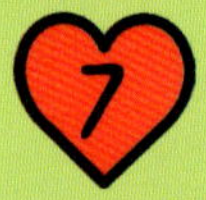

CARNEGIE INTERNATIONAL

"When I paint I liberate monsters."
Pierre Alechinsky

Andrew Carnegie's investment in art institutions certainly worked, spawning Warhol's ground-breaking career and then arguably, Keith's. In 1977 the Carnegie Institute Museum of Art put on a show of the Belgian artist Pierre Alechinsky's work. It blew Keith's mind – suddenly here was an artist with whom he could totally identify. Alechinsky's aesthetic was part folk art, part cartoon, part inspired by Jean Dubuffet. Keith went back again and again. The importance of the show is that it helped Keith identify that he was completely on the right path; as a confidence-booster it was formative. Alechinsky persuaded Keith to make bolder, bigger works. When, quite by chance, an artist dropped out of a big gallery show at the Center for the Arts, the inspired director Audrey Bethel, with great instinct and perspicacity, offered Keith the space. It was, in effect, his first show, convincing him that he could be an artist. It was now time to spread his wings: Keith decided to come clean to Suzy about his sexuality and to head out to New York.

WHERE?
THE CARNEGIE INSTITUTE MUSEUM OF ART, PITTSBURGH.

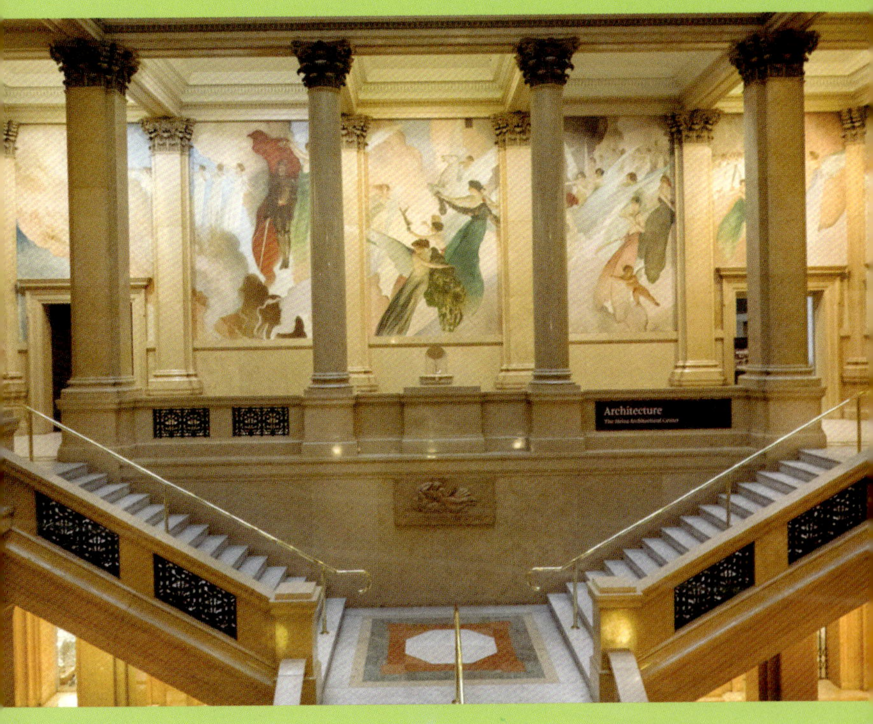
Architecture

EXPERIMENTING

Pittsburgh had shown Keith what he had to do and had given him a nothing-to-lose confidence. Going to New York was entering a world of endless possibilities, fuelled by the fact that here was a city which would allow Keith every opportunity to express his realisation that he was gay. Keith hit the ground running in a rush of sexual and artistic energy, and with the openess to just go for it with a fully open mind. From his art school, SVA (the School of Visual Arts), to the amazing art, music and club scene, much centred on then-edgy Tribeca and the lower east side, Keith just flowed into every new movement, and found himself somehow at the centre of all that was then cool. It was also in New York that he discovered the incredible energy and future significance of the graffiti scene.

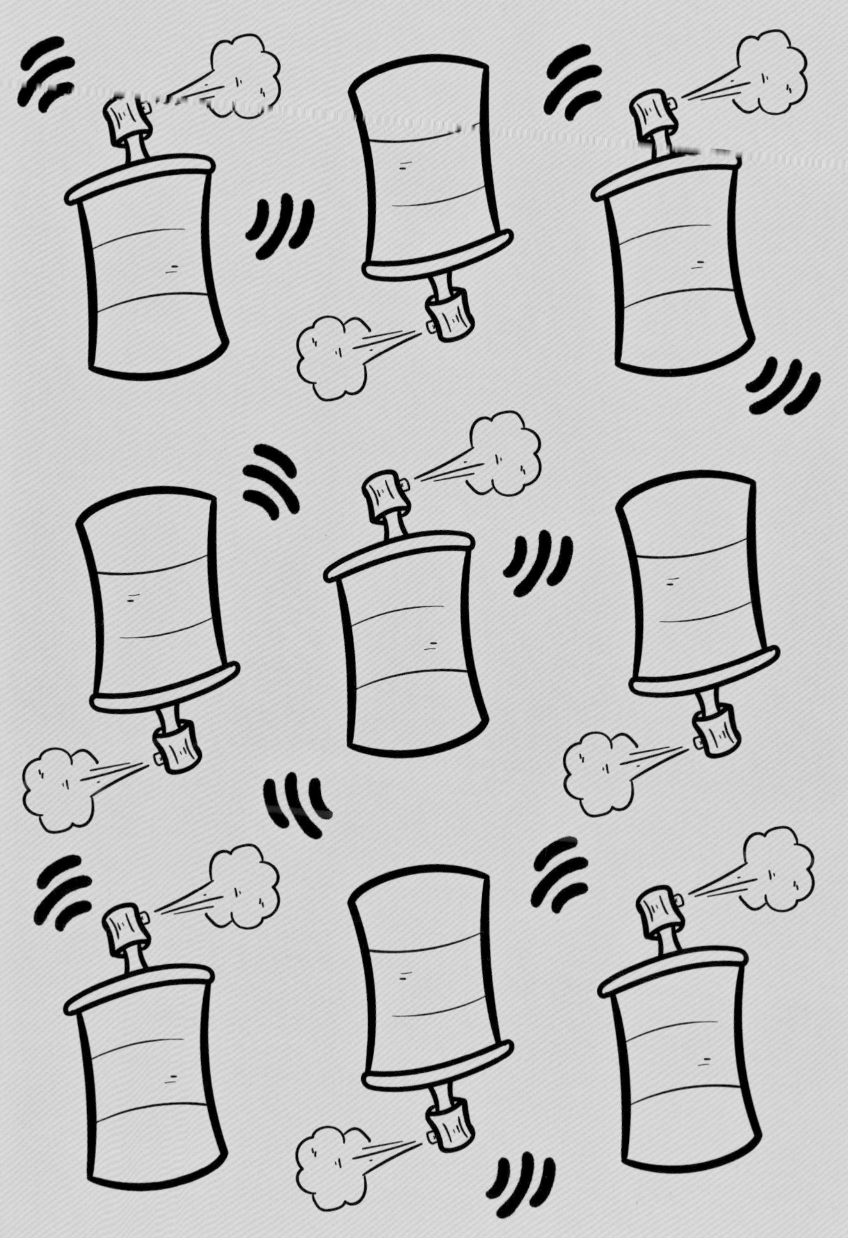

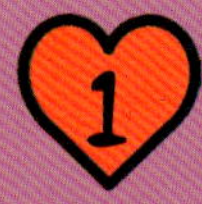

CHRISTOPHER STREET

"Christopher Street...like a candy store."
Keith

Keith knew absolutely no one when he arrived in New York. Like so many newcomers he holed up at the YMCA, then wandered in search of gay bars. Hanging out in Christopher Street, the recognised gay centre of Manhattan, was heaven for Keith. He slid easily into the uninhibited scene, picking someone up and then simply moving in with him a few days later, into a gays-only apartment on West 10th and Bleeker. It was pre-AIDS days and there was sexual freedom in the air. Soon Keith was having anonymous sex in back room bars most nights. Instant friendship, instant sex, an instant place to live. It was, rather like the nature of Keith's art later on, relaxed, immediate and easy.

WHERE?
CHRISTOPHER STREET,
WEST VILLAGE,
MANHATTAN.

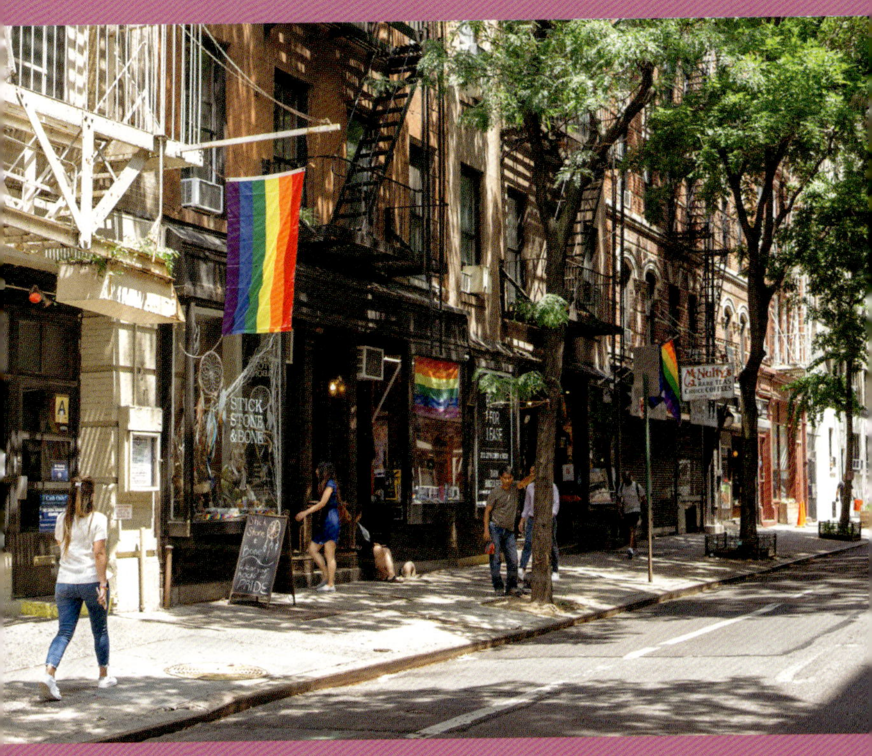
STICK
STONE
& BONE
FOR
LEASE
McNulty's
RARE TEAS
CHOICE COFFEES
PRIDE

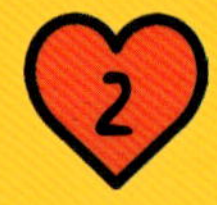

SCHOOL OF VISUAL ARTS

"He was so charming and engaged. He really listened."
Samantha McEwen, fellow student, on Keith.

There was something about Keith that meant that he would just flow in an uncomplicated fashion into things. So arriving at the School of Visual Arts a few days later, Keith did not suffer any existential angst about what he was going to do, or whether he would be a success, or whether he would find his artistic voice. According to his tutors, he was single-minded and determined, asking straight off to borrow spaces so he could cover every surface with paper and try out his patterns. He was witty in a very cartoony way. One assignment involved thinking of an idea and developing it. Keith and his frequently one-track mind produced a big drawing of 300 penises. His contemporaries spoke about his work rate and energy. Others criticised his very commercial way of promoting himself. Yet there was no 'side' to Keith: he was really friendly and approachable. But he wasn't in any way needy. Keith, rather like his linedrawings, seemed to have a clear direction.

WHERE?
SCHOOL OF VISUAL ARTS,
EAST 23RD STREET,
MANHATTAN.

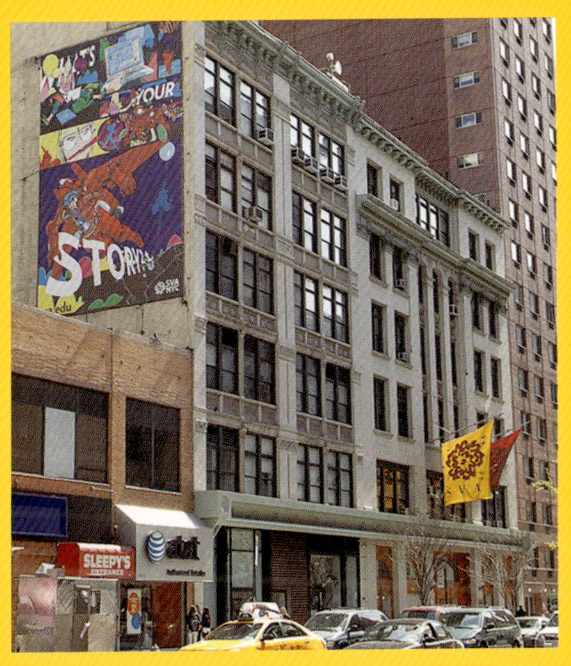
YOUR
STORY
SVA NYC
SLEEPY'S
ENTRANCE

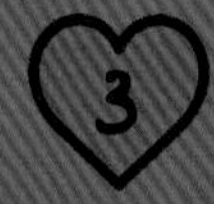

ROCK LOBSTER

"He really had it together...he was so focused." Kenny Scharf

When Drew Straub, a friend from Kutztown, landed in New York with a job as sculptor Kent Floeter's assistant, Keith and Drew moved in together. The apartment was in the East Village, on First Avenue between First and Second Streets. They were both cruising Club Baths, the bath house across the street, sleeping with similar people, but never each other. At SVA Keith was finding energy in pushing the gay thing very directly. At Club Baths he was fascinated by how everyone was sleeping with everyone else in this straightforwardly connected way. One can see the echoes of this in Keith's art of interconnected figures. Drew remembered of their time together that Keith would draw obsessively in their kitchen, often pictures of penises, of men fucking men or dogs: the ruder, the funnier. He would also play the B52s' 'Rock Lobster' over and over and over again. Repetition was becoming a leitmotif to everything Keith was doing: repetitive drawing, cruising every night and music.

WHO?
THE B52'S FIRST ALBUM, FEATURING 'ROCK LOBSTER'.

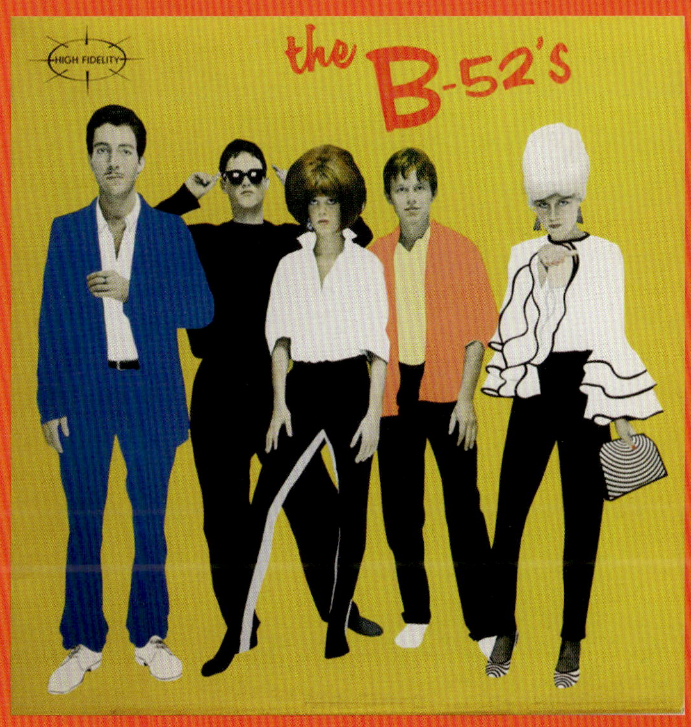
HIGH FIDELITY
the B-52's

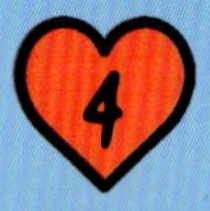

NEW YORK SUBWAY

"We had no idea at that time that...what we were doing was going to be influential."
Keith Haring, the Art Channel

One of the most striking differences between New York and Pittsburgh wasn't just the subway, but more specifically the graffiti both on the outside and inside of subway cars. Keith was instantly struck by the energy, visual inventiveness and originality of this phenomenon, usually created in the poorer outlying neighbourhoods, but brought right into the centre of Manhattan, assailing everyone's senses and sending the NY transport authorities crazy. Where many saw ugliness, Keith saw possibilities. He was struck by the similarities between graffiti and Japanese calligraphy and the 'stream of consciousness' art of Dubuffet and Alechinsky. Keith also saw similarities between his own art, involving spontaneous fluid lines, patterns and bright colours, and the flowing lines of spraycan graffiti. There was something in the air which was resonating with what he was doing. Inadvertently, subway graffiti was validating Keith's artistic direction.

WHERE?
GRAFFITI ON AN NYC SUBWAY CAR.
KEITH LOVED THE RAW ENERGY OF THE GRAFFITI SCENE.

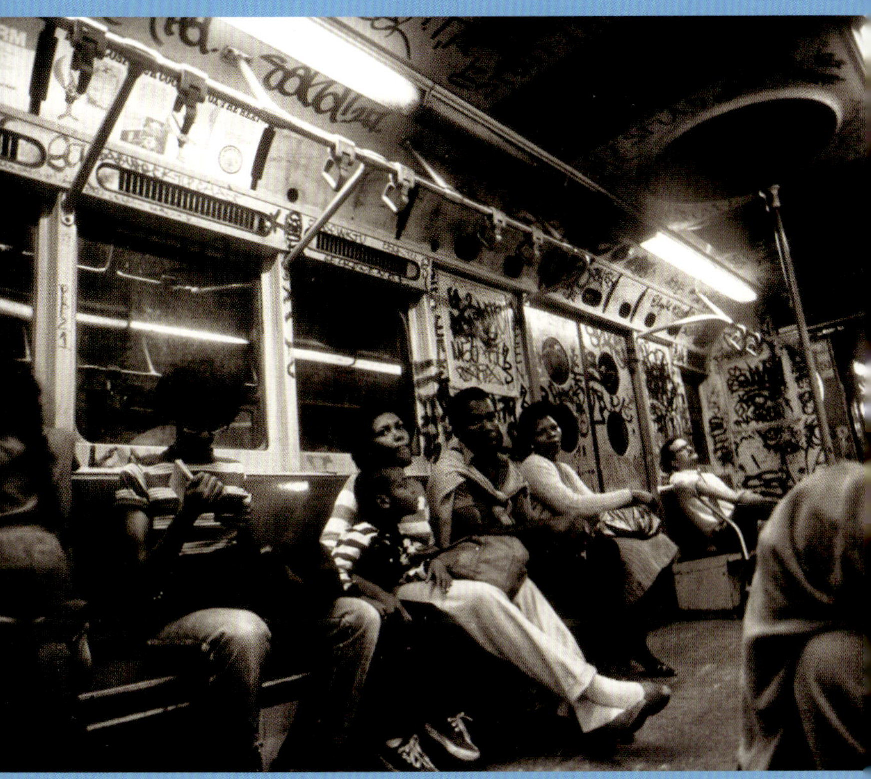

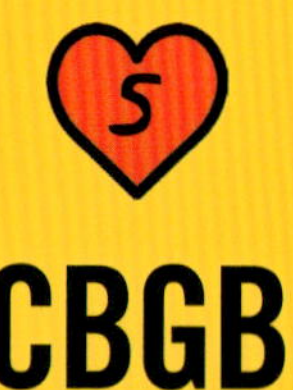

CBGB

"These artists [like Haring] had a new vocabulary to communicate."
Tony Shafrazi

The energy wasn't just in the arts and graffiti scenes but also in music, specifically punk. And in 1978 in New York, punk was transitioning into New Wave, with bands such as Blondie, the Patti Smith Group and the Talking Heads. The venue with which they became synonymous was CBGB's (the acronym stood, bizarrely, for *Country, BlueGrass and Blues*). Keith just became part of the scene – New Wave was about visuals as well as music, and Keith seemed the personification of this new visual energy. More than anything it was another symbol of New York's incredible street culture: music (everyone seemed to be starting a band), visuals, graffiti on the subway, new artists, the burgeoning gay scene in the East Village spilling onto the streets and some amazing new clubs.

WHERE?
CROWDS OUTSIDE CBGB,
315 BOWERY,
MANHATTAN.

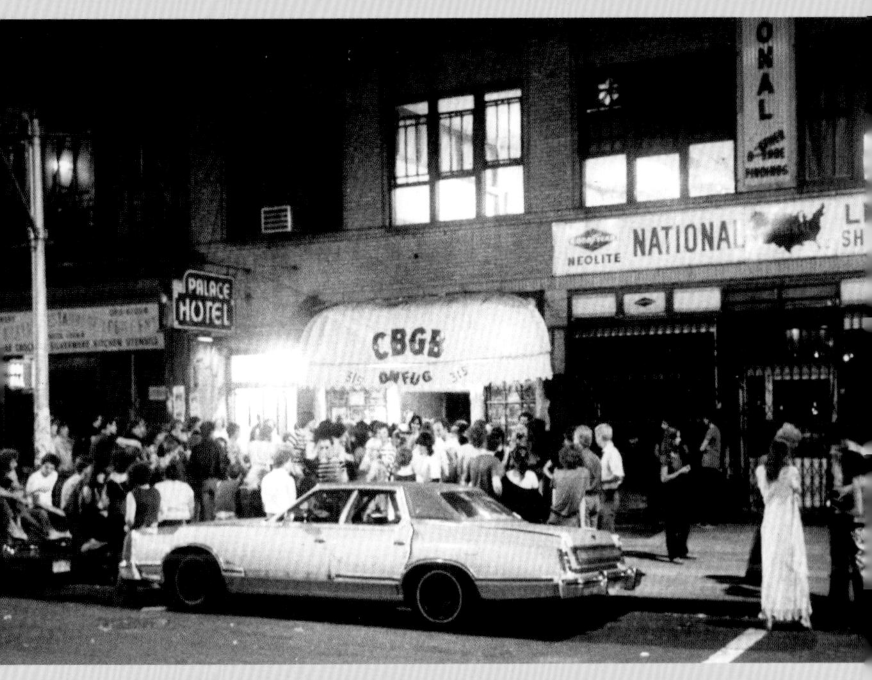
PALACE
HOTEL
CBGB
NEOLITE
NATIONAL

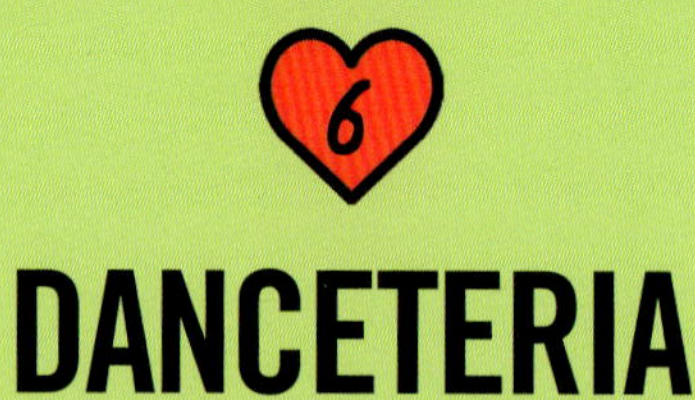

DANCETERIA

"This is the place where anything goes."
Ruth Polsky

Danceteria was where all the downtown crowds, from CBGB, East Village and meatpacking gay bars, and the Mudd Club converged after hours. Keith worked as a bus boy here for a while, and soaked up what was a crossover scene. The dancefloor had been designed by some video artists and was one of the first clubs to have DJs playing whilst videos of random and found footage was projected onto walls. It's easy to forget how innovative the video music scene was then. MTV hadn't got going yet and bands like Blondie and Television were at the forefront of video experimentation. Danceteria hosted gay cabaret acts like Klaus Nomi and it was also where Madonna performed in the very early days and tried out her choreographed ideas. Keith did not try and launch himself as a video artist. But what he did do was somehow soak up a Danceteria vibe almost unfiltered into his work.

WHAT?
DANCETERIA MENU CARD, FEATURING KLAUS NOMI.

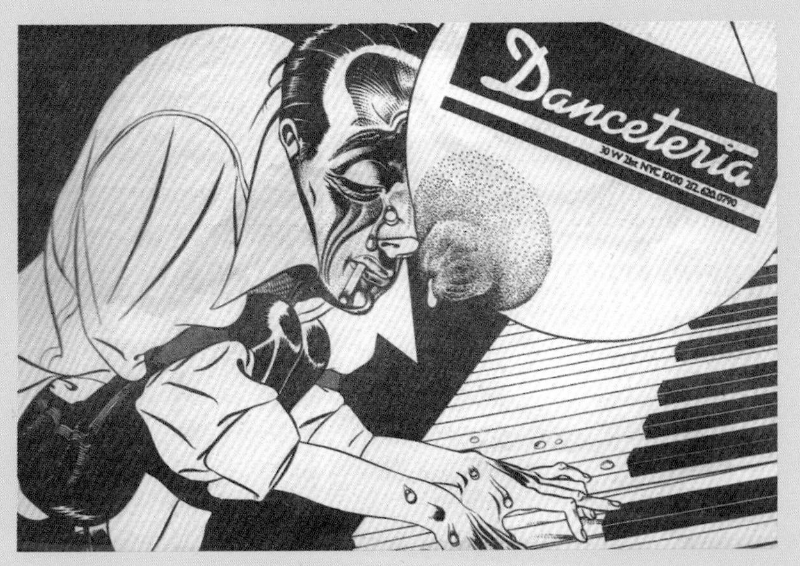
Danceteria
30 W 21st NYC 10010 212.620.0790

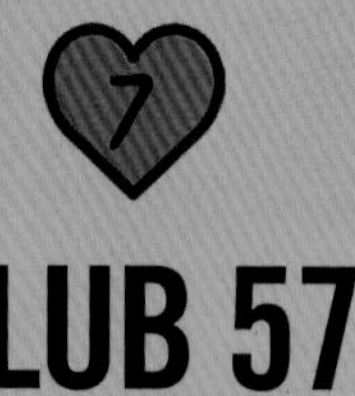

CLUB 57

"It was one big orgy family."
Kenny Scharf

Where Danceteria was a fashionable, very happening scene, the place where the crowd creating new art, music and fashion hung out was Club 57, in the basement of a Polish church on St Mark's Place. Here Keith was with 'family' from SVA – Kenny Scharf, John Sex, Samantha McEwen, Drew Straub and Bruno Schmidt included. Club 57 really was the hangout that began creating the undergound cultural weather. And like Danceteria it was open to all kinds of media. Keith just fell into becoming the art organiser, a sort of curator of the coolest stuff happening underground. And then there was the anything goes pre-AIDS sex – Club 57 had a very bisexual vibe. Keith was totally in his skin and became one of the undisputed leaders of the scene. Of course he was still skint at this point – very few of the crowd had money – but they just knew that they, and by extension Club 57, were the most happening place in NYC.

WHO?
THE POLISH CHURCH AT 57 ST MARK'S PLACE. CLUB 57 HELD ITS OUTRAGEOUS CLUB NIGHTS IN THE BASEMENT.

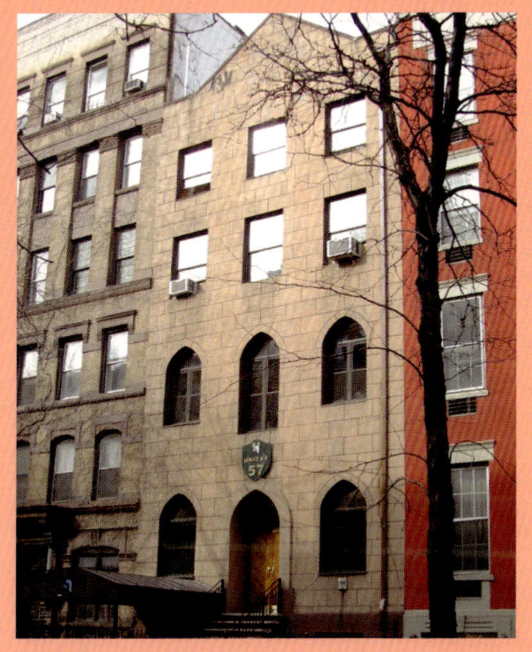

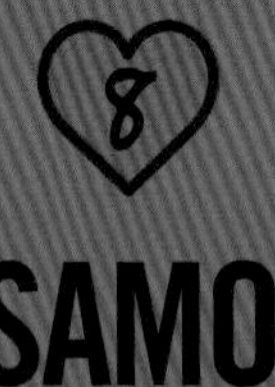

SAMO

"Before I knew who he was, I became obsessed with ...Basquiat's work."
Keith, in Rolling Stone

As Keith was hanging out in the East Village he, along with many others, began noticing this very interesting graffiti – little, short, seemingly meaningless yet striking statements, followed by a '©' symbol and the acronym, SAMO. These were the work of the young Jean-Michel Basquiat, who though not at SVA began to hang around outside, hoping that one of the students would lend him a pass so he could get inside past the security guard. One day, inadevertently, it was Keith who let him in. He was undoubtedly interesting – the conceptual approach to graffiti was fresh and new and intrigued Keith. He in effect became one of Jean-Michel's early patrons, inviting him to exhibit at Club 57. It was typical of the New York scene at the time that two of the future most influential and recognisable artists in the US should meet in this incidental way. Did Jean-Michel influence Keith? Probably not directly, but there are occasional echoes of those short pithy bits of language, a trademark of Basquiat's, in Keith's work.

WHERE?
'SAMO' GRAFFITO BY JEAN-MICHEL BASQUIAT IN THE EAST VILLAGE, MANHATTAN.

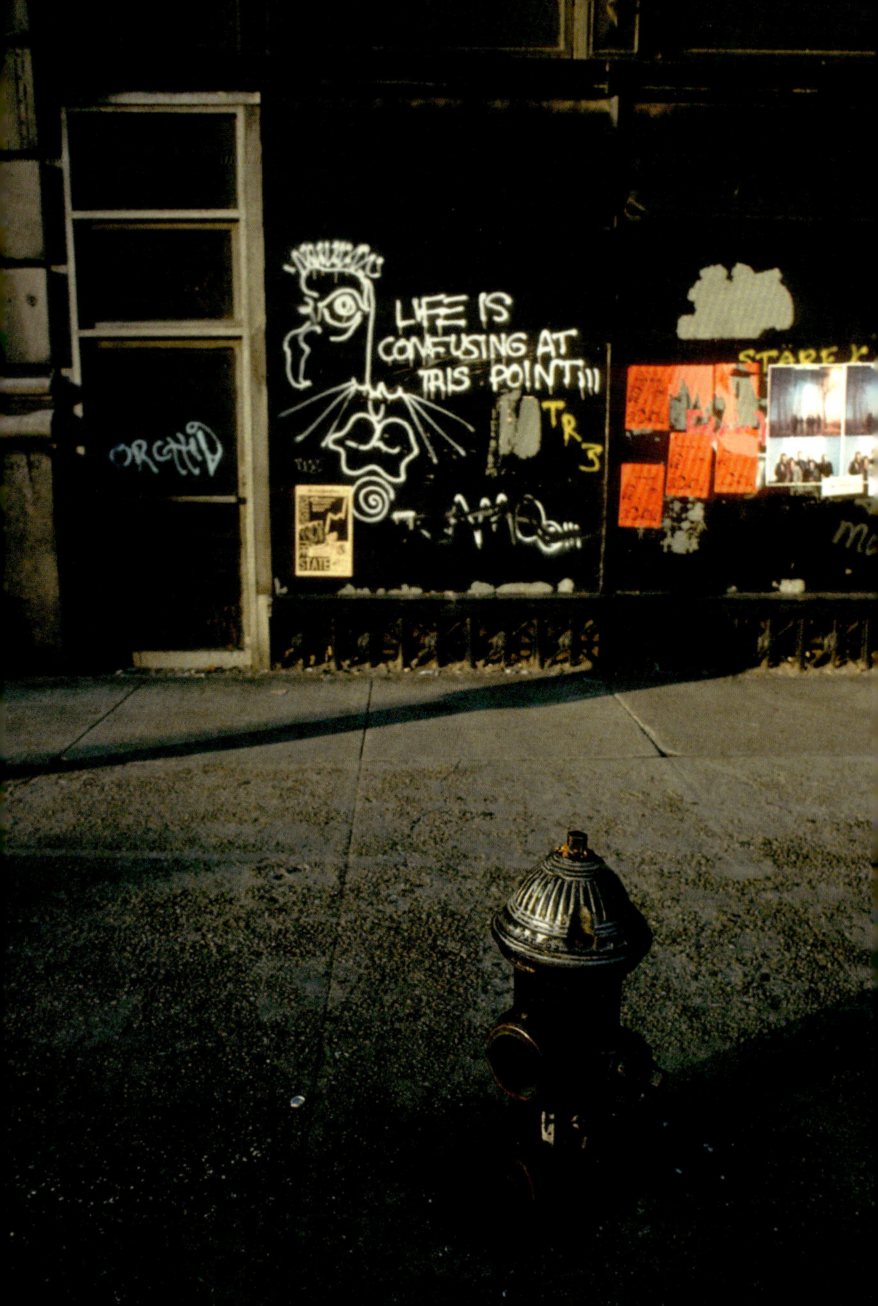
LIFE IS
CONFUSING AT
THIS POINT!!!
ORCHID

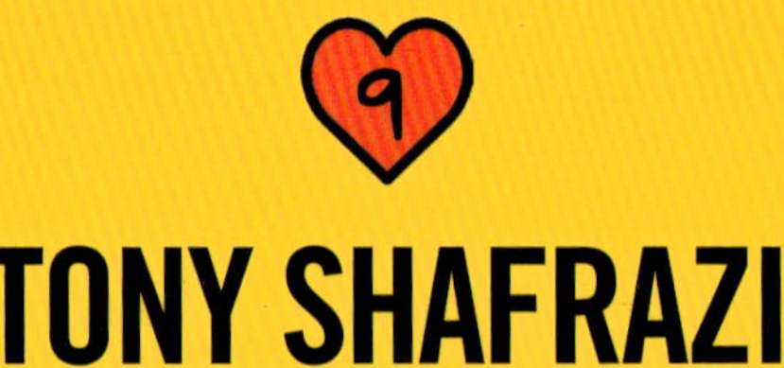

TONY SHAFRAZI

"Warhol is the father of these artists who also seek a direct engagement with the public." **The Art Channel**

Like many other artists, Basquiat included, Keith was always short of money and needed to odd jobs to keep going in NYC. One job involved him picking wild flowers from the New Jersey turnpike, to sell to restaurants back in Manhattan. Another was to prove life-changing. Keith went to work as an assistant to the naughty-boy art dealer (he achieved notoriety by spraying "Kill Lies All" on a Picasso at MOMA in 1974) Tony Shafrazi. Working for Tony gave Keith real insights into the gallery world. He hated the asinine nature of much of that scene and committed to plugging into the underground. Shafrazi helped to crystallize Keith's conviction that the new art could exist outside the gallery system. Keith was also starting to get the huge significance of Andy Warhol. Shortly afterwards he also decided that it was time to quit SVA. There were more part-time jobs, including as a bicycle courier. Simultaneously Keith was curating more happening art shows at Club 57.

WHO?
TONY SHAFRAZI OUTSIDE HIS SOHO (MERCER STREET) GALLERY.

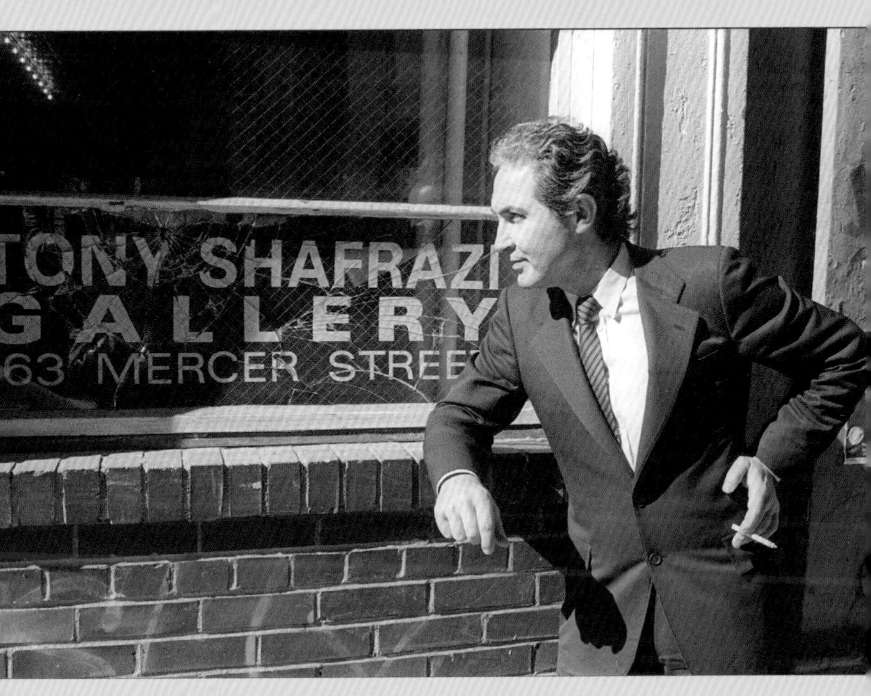
TONY SHAFRAZI
GALLERY
63 MERCER STREET

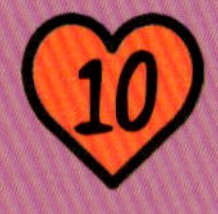

THE MUDD CLUB

"Often times it was just a beautiful mess."
Richard Boch, ex Mudd Club doorman

All the inspired new stuff that Keith was doing at Club 57 out of simple enthusiasm bore fruit when Steve Maas offered Keith a job doing the same at the Mudd Club. Mass, an aspiring film-maker, opened the six floor club with art curator Diego Cortez and 'It' girl Anya Phillips, with a concert by the B-52s. It quickly became established as the place to hang in Manhattan after CBGBs. The cocktail of drugs, dancing, sex and art, curated by Keith on the fourth floor, was irresistible. It started attracting Manhattan's coolest crowd, including Andy Warhol, David Bowie, Debbie Harry, Allen Ginsberg, Klaus Nomi, David Byrne, Basquiat and his then girlfriend Madonna. Again Keith somehow found himself in the middle of the hippest scene in the city. At this point he was taking a lot of cocaine, which kept him going until 4 am, when, after another line, he would typically go to the gay S&M club, The Anvil.

WHERE?
MUDD CLUB INTERIOR,
77 WHITE STREET,
TRIBECA.
CABARET STAR KLAUS NOMI IN THE FOREGROUND.

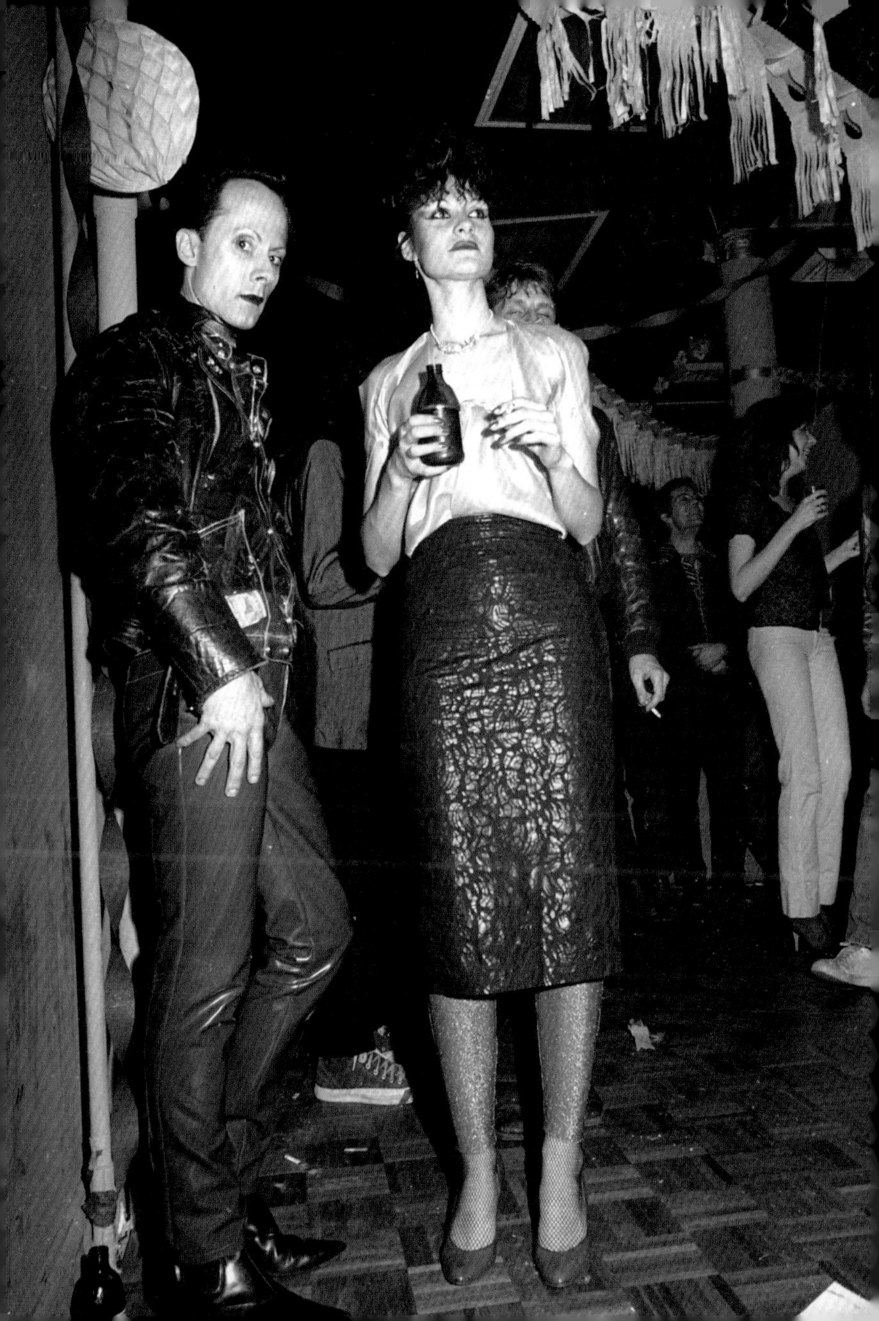

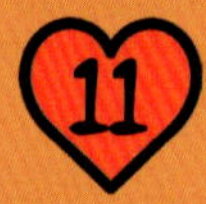

THE TIMES SQ SHOW

"This show proves there are no classes in art, no differentiation."
John Ahearn, COLAB curator

Maybe it was luck, but Keith seemed to have a talent for always being in the right place at the right time. He had already clocked Basquiat and his SAMO graffiti. He had done a little himself in the East Village – some faked posters bearing the message 'Clones Go Home' – aimed at yuppies starting to muscle in on the edgy gay neighbourhood. Now he started experimenting with his own tags, featuring what would become his signature barking dog and baby images. With his graffiti credentials and his underground art connections established, Keith was invited to show at what would prove to be a breakthrough show: the COLAB–organised Times Square Show, also featuring Jean-Michel Basquiat, Fab 5 Freddy (of 'Rapture' fame), Jenny Holzer and Nan Goldin. Keith did a painting with hundreds of pink penises. The influence of the show was dramatic, transforming the New York art scene. Very soon serious galleries began to see that graffiti had the energy to take art in a new direction and that there were big profits to be made from the shift.

WHERE?
THE SEEDY TIMES SQUARE NEIGHBOURHOOD IN 1980.
THE COLAB SHOW WAS HELD IN AN EX-PORN SHOP.

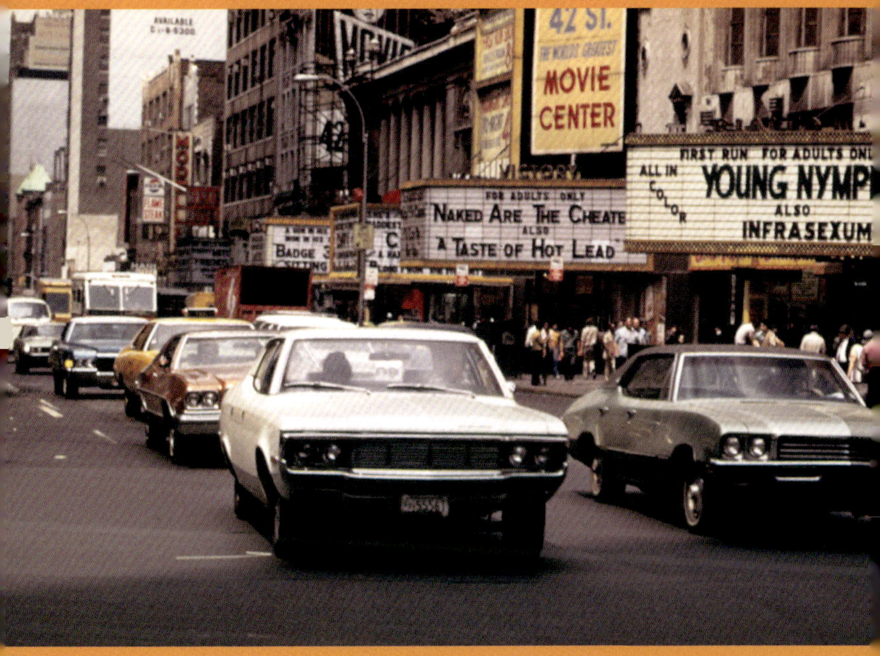

42 St.
THE WORLD'S GREATEST
MOVIE
CENTER
VICTORY
FOR ADULTS ONLY
Naked Are The Cheate
ALSO
A Taste of Hot Lead
FIRST RUN FOR ADULTS ONL
ALL IN COLOR
YOUNG NYMP
ALSO
INFRASEXUM
BADGE 3

KEITH HARING'S USA

Keith was so involved with his art that he had little time to explore the USA. From his birth in small-town Kutztown, it was Pittsburgh and then straight to New York. Manhattan had everything he ever wanted – a fun and outrageous gay scene, the best clubs at that point on the planet, some brilliant art dealers and a sense of freedom. Travel within the US was almost always related to work. When he wasn't in New York, Keith tended to be in Europe or Japan.

❶ Kutztown
Keith spent his childhood years here, but soon got bored of its small-town values.

❷ Pittsburgh
Pittsburgh opened up the possibilities of art to Keith and gave him his first show. Andy Warhol, a previous son of Pittsburgh, also proved a great inspiration.

❸ New York
The moment Keith arrived in the city, he felt instantly in his skin. He immediately came out and became a very active member of the gay scene. New York had everything Keith needed to thrive – SVA, a fantastic art school, a graffiti scene for inspiration, an amazingly creative crowd centred around clubs like Mudd and Club57, and avid collectors and dealers interested in his art. Once he'd arrived, Keith only ever wanted to live in Manhattan, around Soho and the East Village. It was in Manhattan that he died.

❹ Philadelphia
As part of his engagement with kids, Keith created a collaborative mural in the city in 1987.

❺ Iowa City
Keith created some murals here, for the Ernest Horn School in 1989.

❻ Chicago
Keith came here to do a fabulous collaborative mural with children from several Chicago public schools in 1989.

❼ Los Angeles
Haring spent very little time in LA. He did make a trip in 1989, together with his companion, and created a mural in Pasadena. However he was surprisingly friendly with some significant Hollywood stars, who had become collectors after seeing his work in NYC.

LOCATIONS WITH HARING SCULPTURES:

❶ Grand Rapids, MI
❷ Kutztown, PA
❸ New York, NY
❹ Dobbs Ferry, NY
❺ St Louis, MO
❻ San Francisco, CA

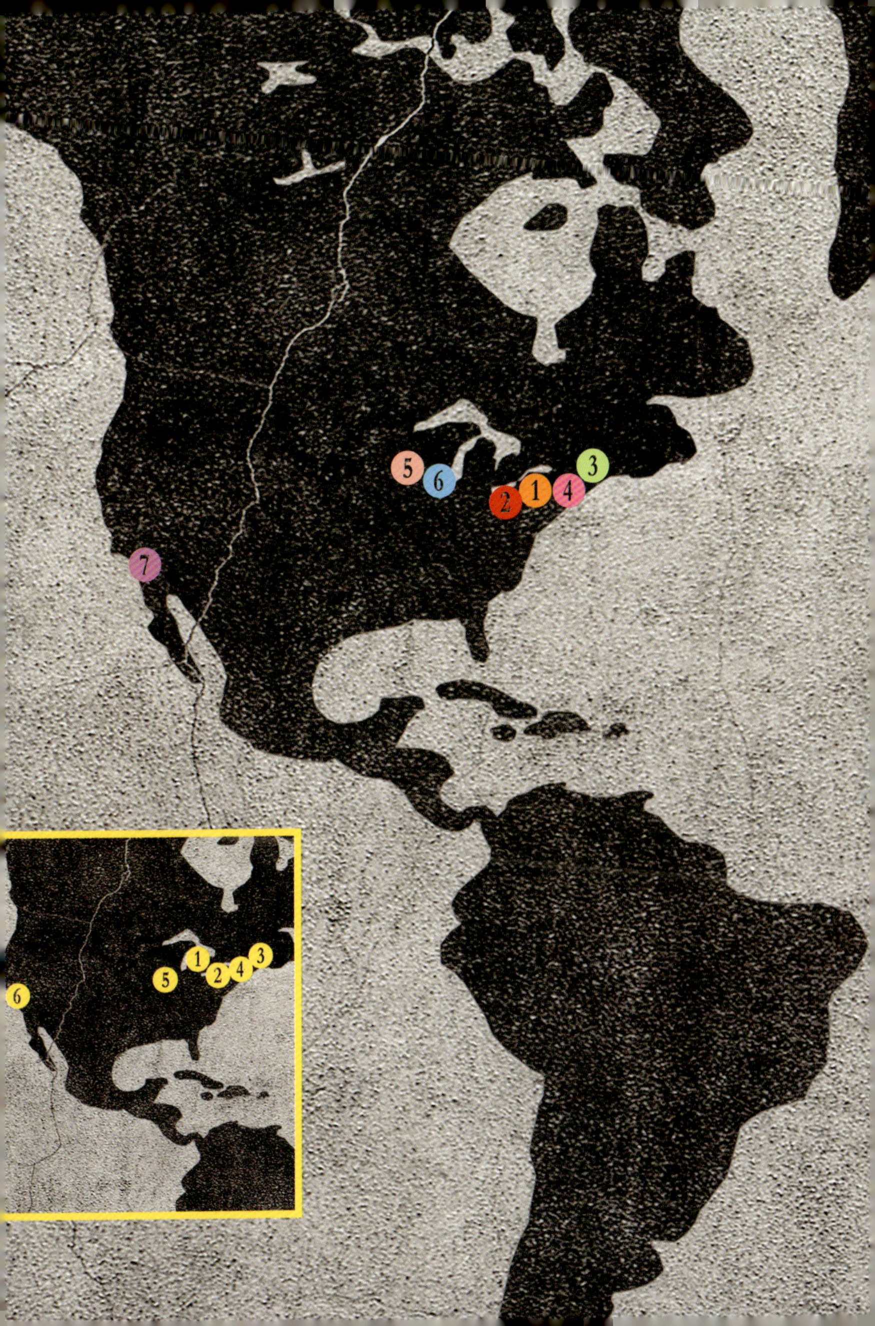
5
6
2
1
4
3
7
1
3
5
2
4
6

TAKE OFF

The speed at which Keith's career took off after the Times Square show was, by any measure, extraordinary. Not for him the early incomprehension that Warhol faced, or Basquiat scratching for a few dollars by selling postcards and T-shirts of his work. Keith quickly acquired two powerful collectors, Donald and Mera Rubell. He didn't chase them; they came to find him. It was the same with the dealers: they came calling. Aged only 24 Keith had a hugely successful solo show at the serious Shafrazi gallery. And then the money started to flow. From being bankable in Manhattan, he also found huge demand for what he was doing in Kassel, Amsterdam, Zurich, Naples, Tokyo and London. Everyone wanted a piece of Keith, not least Andy Warhol, Bowie, Malcolm McLaren, Vivienne Westwood and Grace Jones.

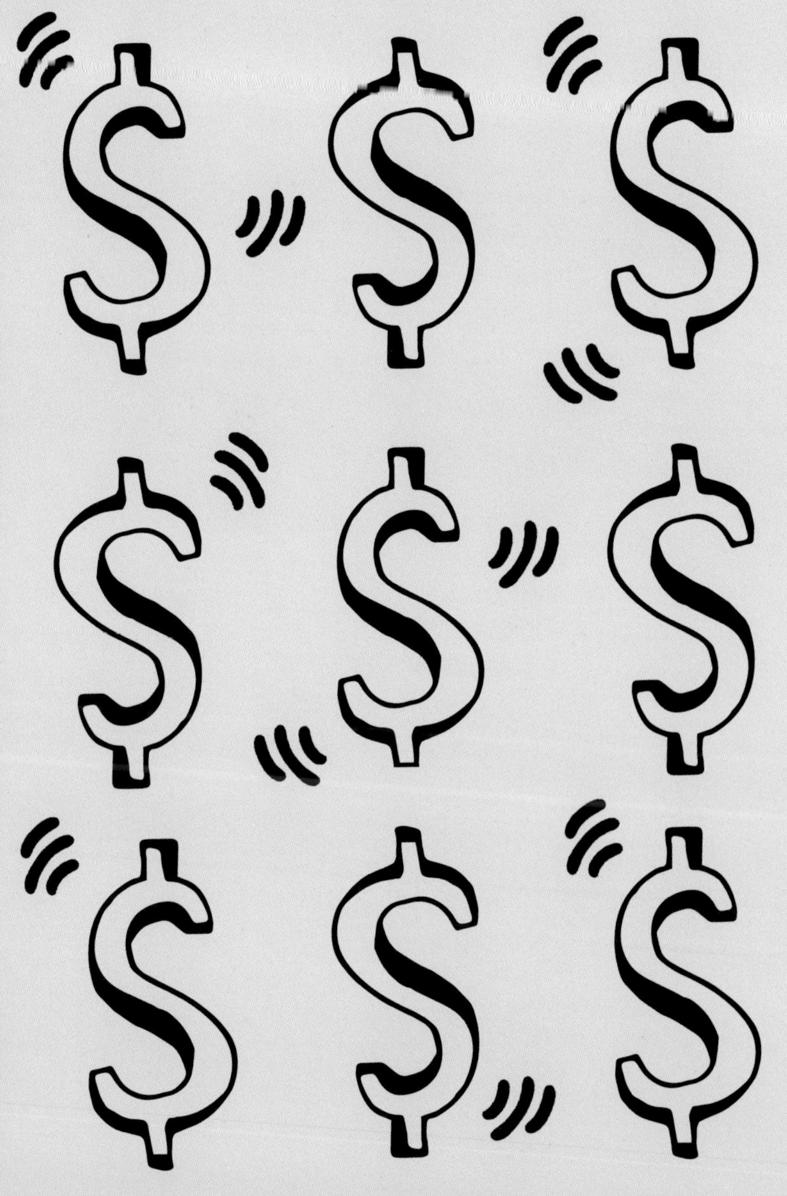

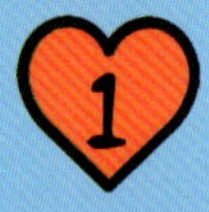

THE NYC SUBWAY

***"As graffiti artists say...he wanted eyeballs."* Carlos Rodriguez on Keith.**

Keith became good friends with Fab 5 Freddy and they started checking out graffiti in New York's 'Alphabet City' – the then no-go, druggy Lower East Side streets of Avenues A, B, C and D. But, whilst he was inspired by the streets, Keith's real contribution to the scene was on the subway. He had long admired the energy of NYC graffiti artists risking arrest by spraying the insides and outsides of subway cars, creating a sort of moving art gallery of their work. But Keith had other ideas. He had noticed blank black advertising panels, awaiting new posters, and realised they made a perfect canvas. Soon, using chalk (minimal damage), he started covering them with his signature barking dogs, babies and other figures. They became notorious, with people looking forward to Keith's new work. He started treating it almost as a job, doing 40 or 50 drawings a day on pre-determined routes. Keith also cleverly got his Mudd Club friend, photographer Tseng Kwong Chi, to photograph every new image. Henry Geldzahler, Culture Commissioner for NYC, got to hear of the project and logged the fact that something new and very interesting was emerging.

WHERE?
KEITH PAINTING ONE OF HIS NOTORIOUS IMAGES ON AN NYC SUBWAY BLANK ADVERTISING PANEL

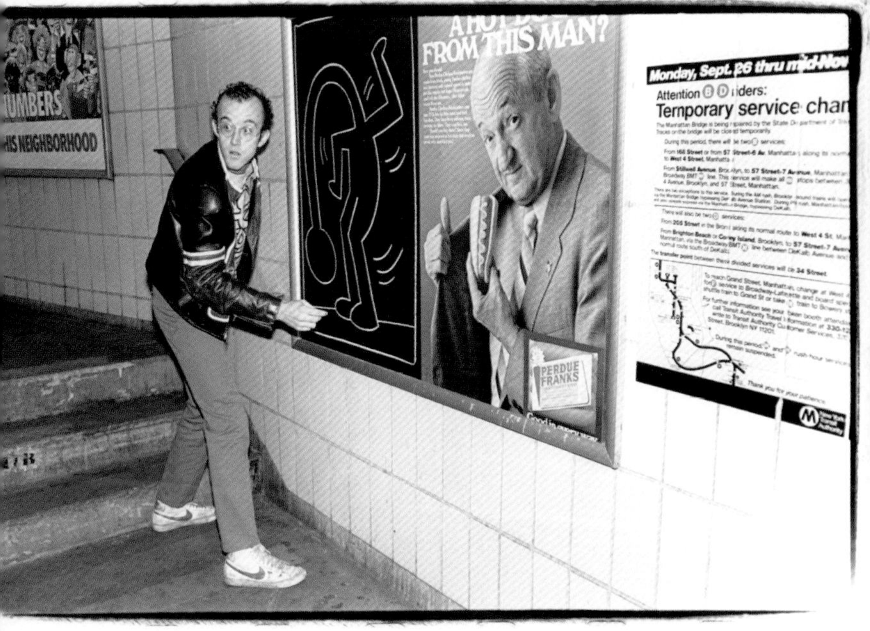

UMBERS
HIS NEIGHBORHOOD
FROM THIS MAN?
PERDUE FRANKS
Monday, Sept. 26 thru mid-Nov
Attention riders:
Temporary service char

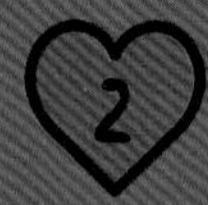

BEYOND WORDS

"The first time a South Bronx hip-hop show was seen downtown." Viral Art Blog

At this point in his career Keith was as significant for his curation as for his art: he arguably gave more exposure to graffiti as art than anyone else. Fab 5 Freddy had introduced him to a group of uptown graffiti artists who were also part of the hip-hop scene, and Keith hit upon the idea of putting on a show of as much of the graffiti scene, both uptown and downton, as possible, at the Mudd Club. He made Fab 5 and Futura 2000 guest curators. The show was a riot of talent and energy, but also started getting out of hand with the whole club being tagged by the featured artists and their friends. From thinking it was a great idea, Steve Mass, the owner of Mudd, decided it was too much, with neighbours complaining and threatening to close the whole club down. Haring had gone too far and the prospect of being fired hung over him. Instead of waiting for Mass, he decided to quit. Significantly he had sold his first drawings a few days earlier. The prospect of being able to support himself through his art suddenly seemed real.

WHO?
FAB 5 FREDDY (ON LEFT) WITH JEAN-MICHEL BASQUIAT.

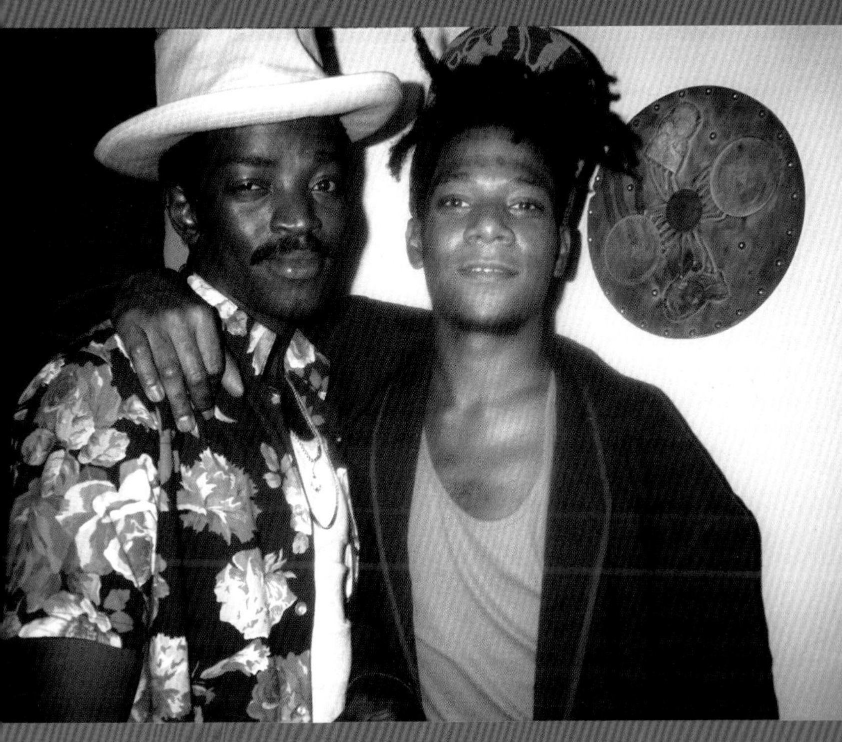

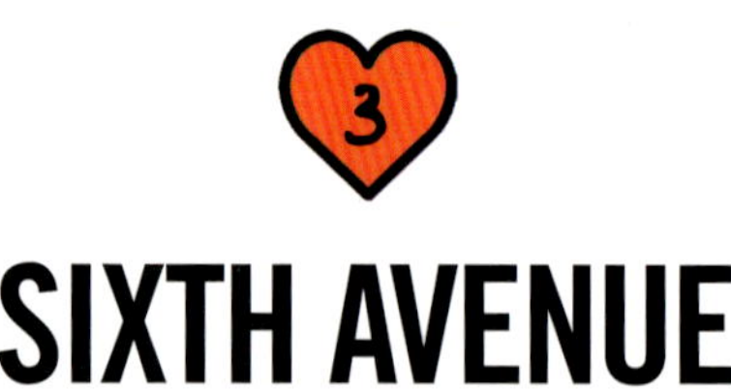

SIXTH AVENUE

"They were forward and fierce in their choices." **Richard Prince on the Rubells as collectors.**

Kenny Scharf, Keith's friend from SVA, had moved into an ex-photographer's two storey loft, on Sixth Avenue near Bryant Park, and soon Keith joined him, taking the top floor. It was whilst living here that Keith acquired his first patrons: Donald and Mera Rubell. Don, an obstetrician, and Mera, then a preschool teacher, started collecting young artists whilst Don was still at medical school, supported by Mera. They had first met Keith at the Mudd Club Beyond Words show, and followed up, as was their habit, by visiting him in his loft studio, where they bought a few works. To Kenny's frustration, they did not buy any of his – he found success as an artist later on. The Rubells were at the head of a wave of enthusiasm for Keith's work, and with their support behind him, Keith was effectively launched. Over time the Rubells would own over 80 Harings.

WHO?
KENNY SCHARF, KEITH'S FELLOW STUDENT FROM SVA, AND ROOM MATE.

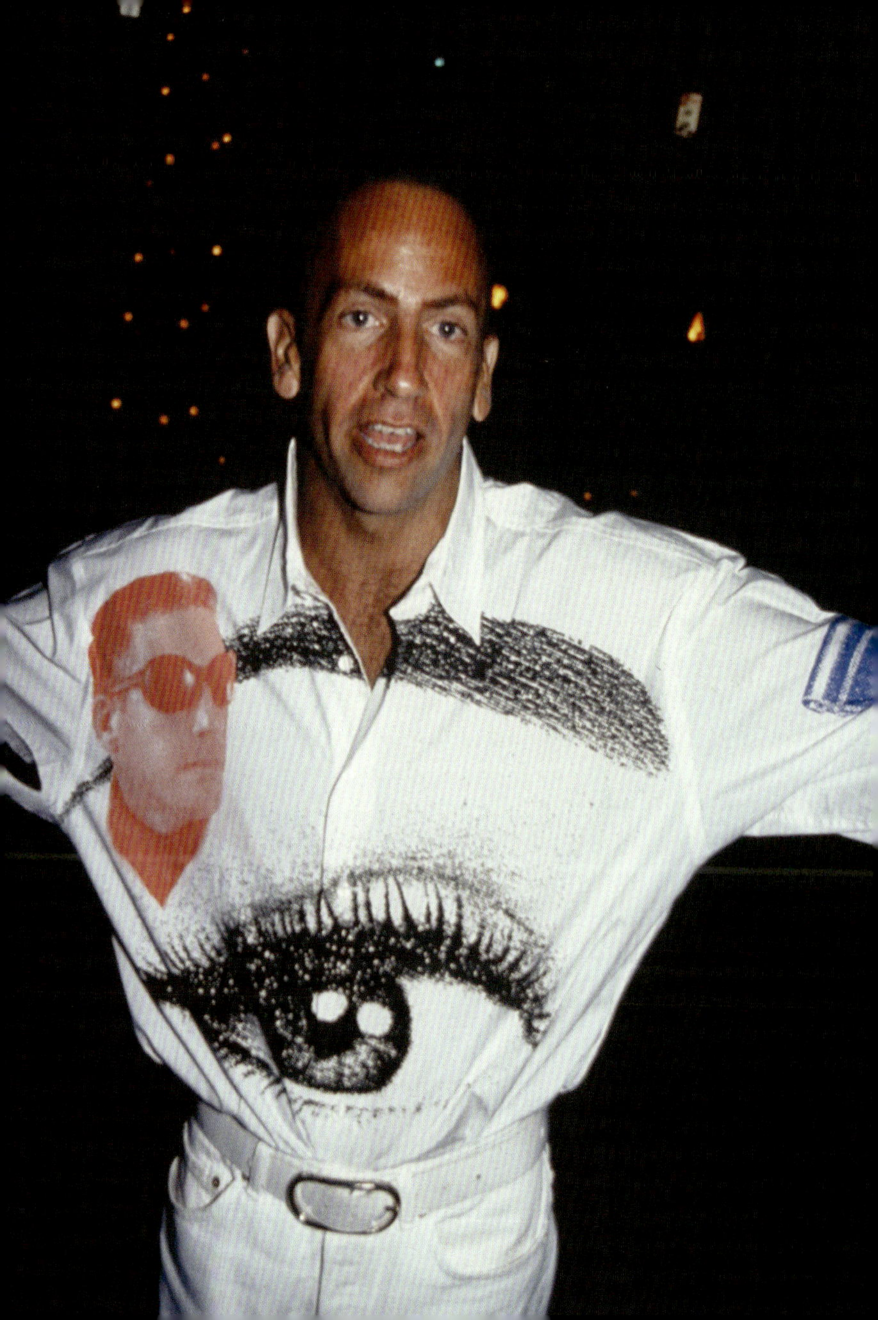

BROOME STREET

"Jean...did all the cooking for Keith, he sort of kept house so Keith could work."

Samantha McEwen

Tensions between Keith and Kenny Scharf, as well as the latter's split from his long-term girlfriend Samantha McEwen, would lead to Keith moving out of Sixth Avenue and into a loft in Broome Street with Samantha. It was at this time that Keith first really fell in love, with Jean Dubose, a DJ from Dominica, who he met cruising St Marks Baths. Jean then moved in. Keith loved his company and the sex (not entirely monogamous: they both had an understanding), but also Jean's excellent cooking. The apartment had interconnecting rooms but no corridor, meaning Samantha had to go through the boys' bedroom to get to the kitchen. Keith came up with a brilliant solution – he and Jean pitched a tent, which became their bedroom and allowed everyone some privacy. Keith then also rented the basement at Broome Street, to use as a studio. His life was now rather settled – working in the studio, or out creating his subway pieces, hanging with Fab 5 Freddy or his new friend, graffiti artist LA II (a.k.a. Angel Ortiz), coming home to Jean's cooking and lots of coke and sex.

WHERE?
LOFTS IN BROOME STREET, SOHO, MANHATTAN.

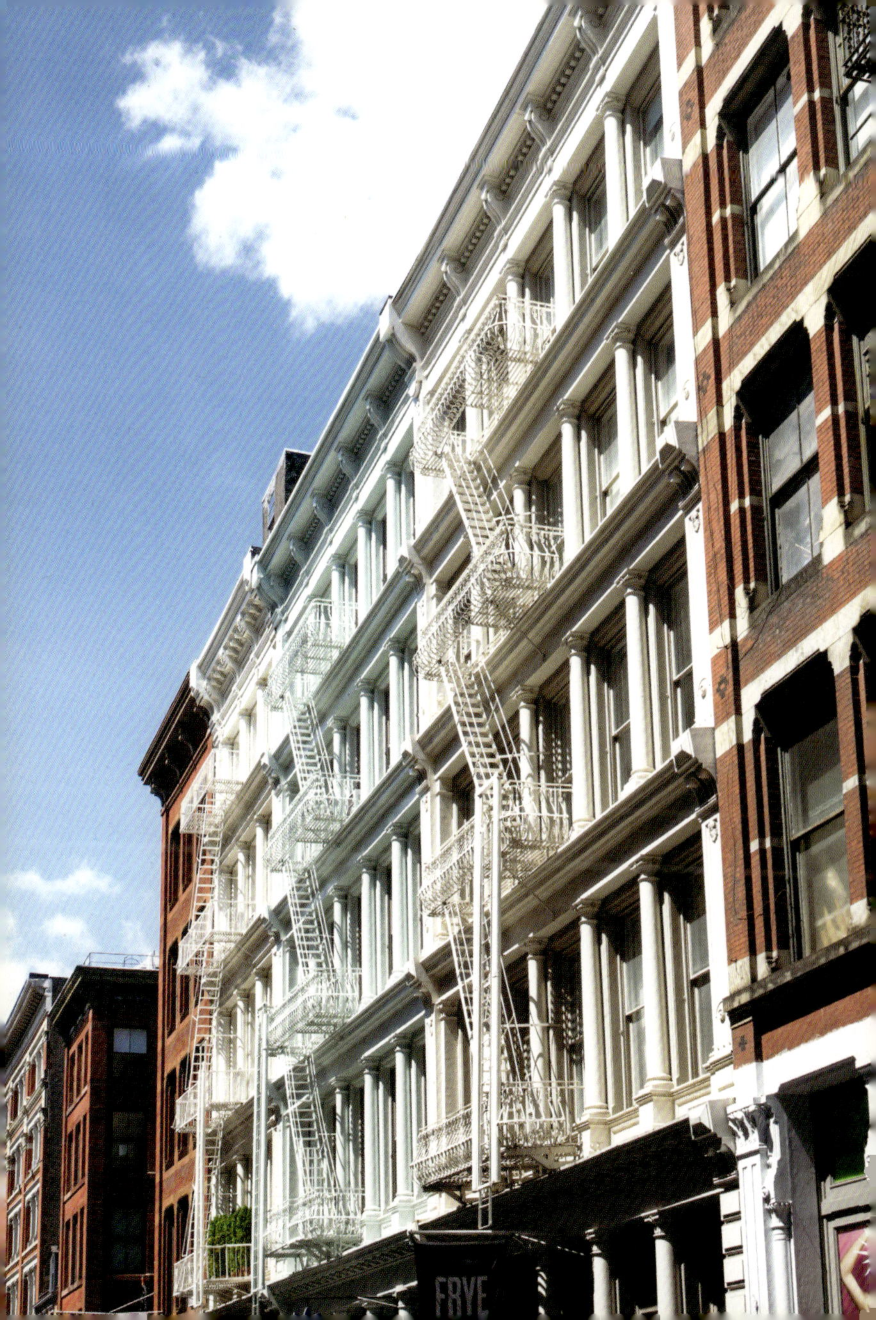
FRYE

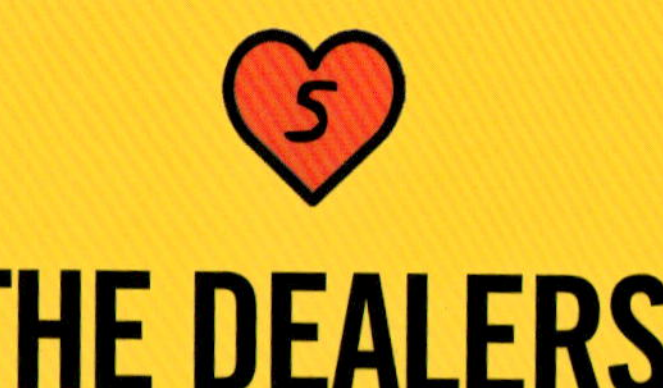

THE DEALERS

"It's culture or it's not culture."
Annina Nosei, art dealer

There was nothing like a buzz to get New York art dealers salivating and, with several private collectors going to buy Harings at his loft, the dealers were not far behind. The clever NYC Culture Commissioner Henry Geldzahler, who had already clocked Keith, then went to see him at Broome Street. He was hugely impressed and, back in his office, encouraged his staff to go and buy a picture. How many did is unrecorded, but soon the dealers were calling. Keith had, idealistically, been anti the gallery system, but realising how nauseating dealing with some punters could be, decided that maybe they had their uses. Among those to visit were the smart Annina Nosei (who was representing Basquiat), Brooke Alexander (dealing in Ruscha, Richard Tuttle and Donald Judd) and Tony Shafrazi, for whom Keith had worked as an assistant. To add to Keith's marketability, he was starting to get arrested for his drawings on the subway. In the end Shafrazi, the rebel who had himself, as an anti-Vietnam protest, slightly defaced Picasso's *Guernica* at MOMA in his youth, was Keith's choice.

WHO?
ITALIAN-BORN NYC POWER DEALER, ANNINA NOSEI, IN HER GALLERY. SHE TOO SPOTTED KEITH'S TALENT EARLY.

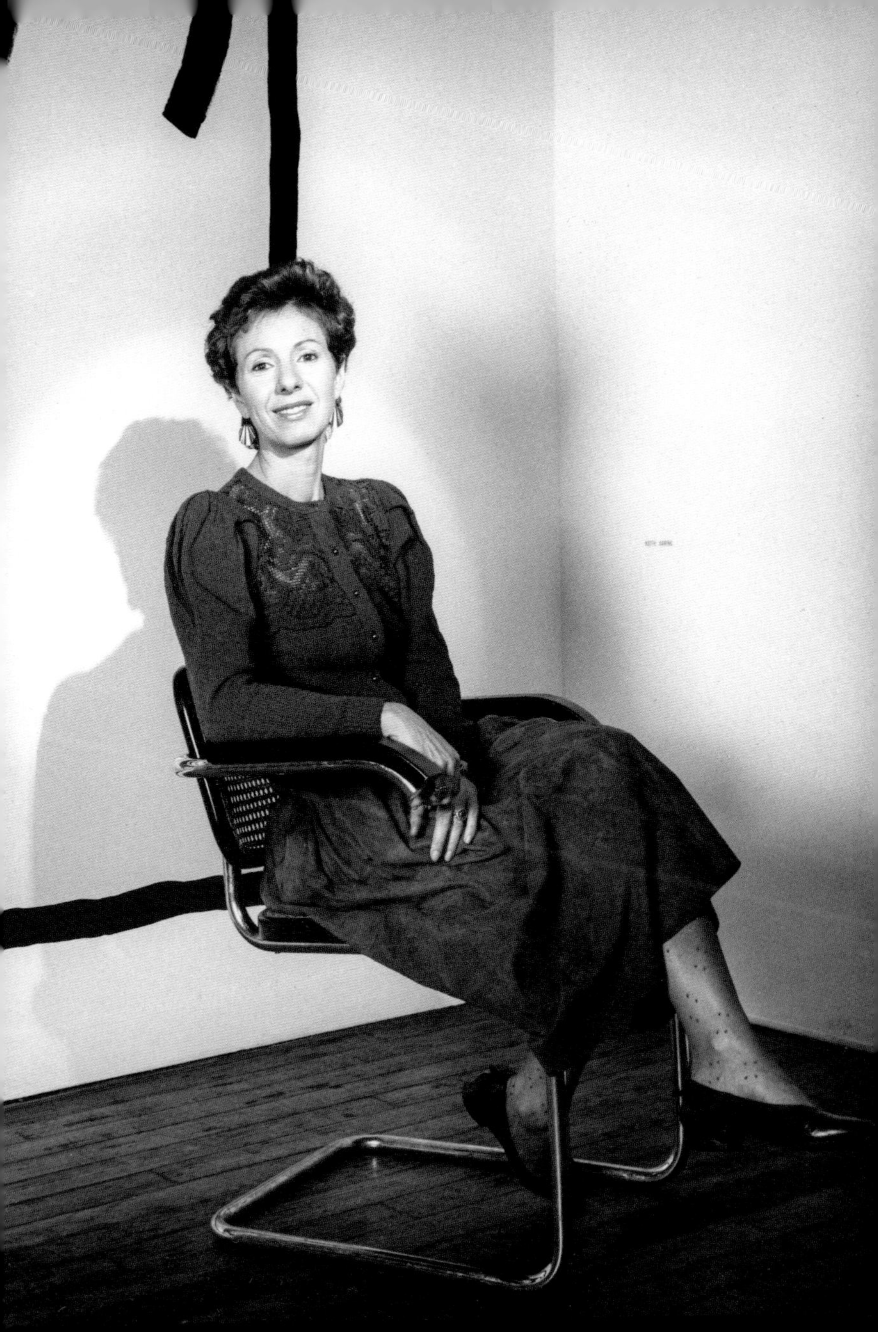

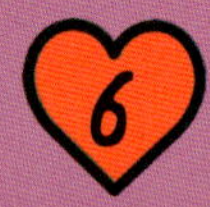

TONY SHAFRAZI 2

"By 1982, with his first one man exhibition... he had become an international art star."

Tony Shafrazi, on Keith

Shafrazi recognised Keith's genius and the timing was right: he was planning a new gallery space in then edgy Soho, at 163 Mercer Street, and offered Keith a solo show that October. Keith created a series of huge works on building tarpaulins. LA II helped decorate the pillars in the gallery. Shafrazi and Haring produced an expensive book for the show, with a celebratory essay by the critic Jeffrey Deitch entitled *Why the Dogs are Barking.*The buzz was palpable, with Keith in action being filmed by CBS Evening News. On opening night the gallery was mobbed: graffiti artists, fine artists (including Lichtenstein, Serra, Rauschenberg and Clemente) and, of course, the Rubells. It was a real happening and a critical and commercial success. Haring prices now started going up and Keith felt flush. It had all happened so quickly – he was only 24.

WHO?
KEITH, IN CONFIDENT FORM, SHORTLY AFTER HIS FIRST SHAFRAZI SHOW.

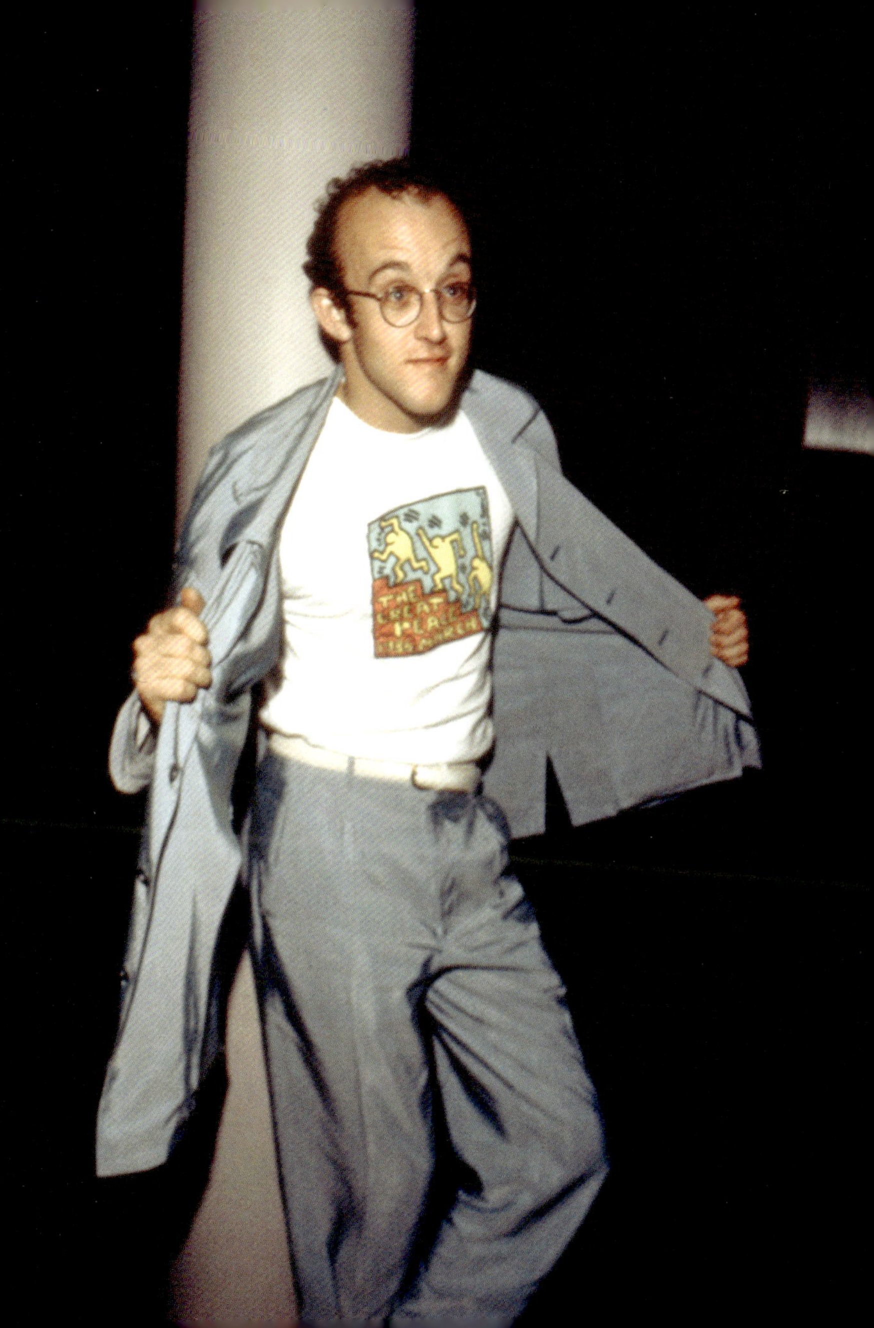

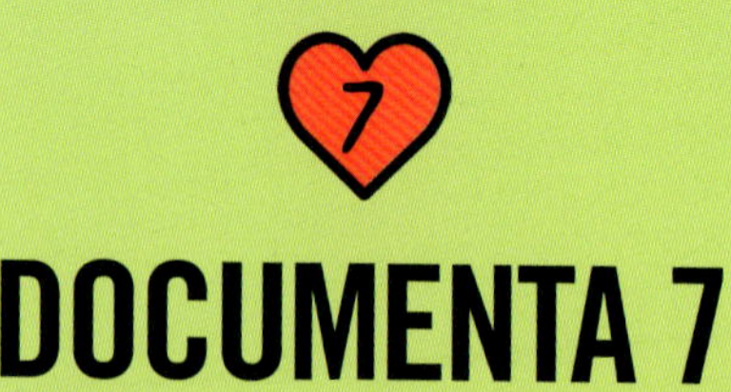

DOCUMENTA 7

"The [1980s] witnessed the emergence of... the international art market and a gallery system that 'lusted after' salable works."

Documenta.de

Rudi Fuchs, the Dutch Artistic Director of Documenta, a quinquennial art show held at the stunning Fridericianum in Kassel, was very savy at picking up on new talent. He was across what was going on in New York and, perfect timing again, he invited Keith to show his huge tarp paintings from the Shafrazi Gallery at his forthcoming, prestigious Documenta show. Keith was seemingly effortlessly joining art aristocracy on an international level. Also showing at Documenta 7 were Carl Andre, Giovanni Anselmo, Georg Baselitz, Basquiat, Joseph Beuys, Francesco Clemente, Donald Judd, Claes Oldenburg, Gerhard Richter, Cindy Sherman, Cy Twombly, Andy Warhol...the list goes on. And it was, almost naïvely, only Keith's second time in Europe, a few weeks after his first, a short trip to Rotterdam and Amsterdam. More importantly big money was entering the art market and Haring was in demand. His prices were going up, up, up.

WHERE?
THE FRIDERICIANUM,
FRIEDRICHSPLATZ, KASSEL.

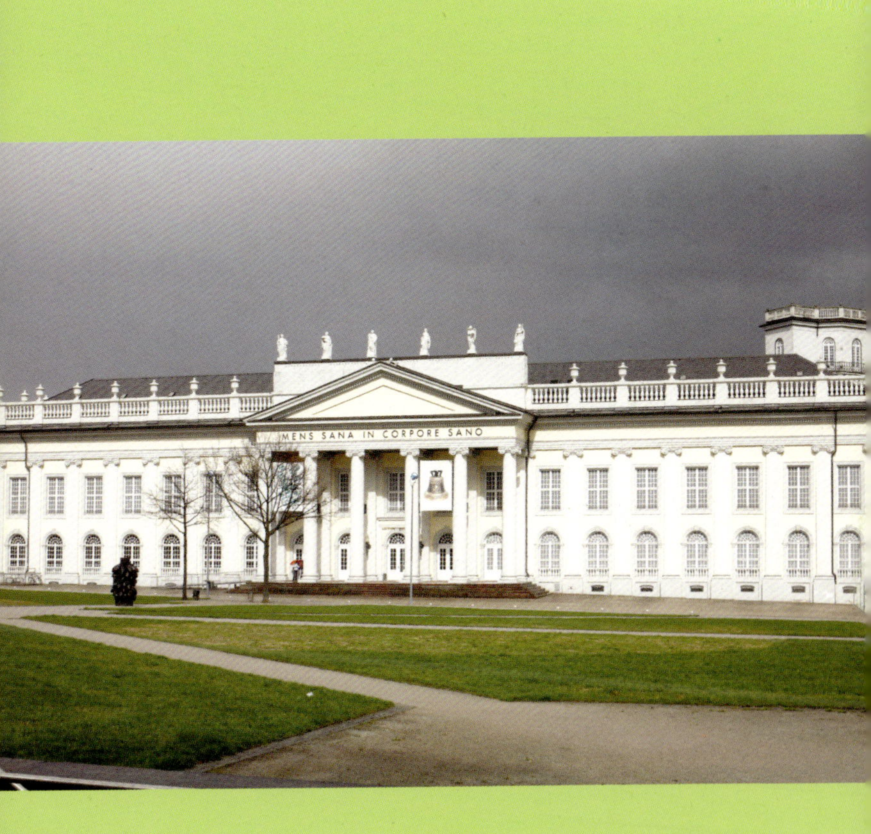
MENS SANA IN CORPORE SANO

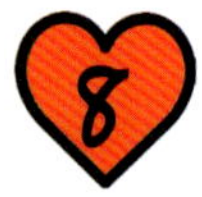

THE FUN GALLERY

"A place where...downtown artists... mixed with museum directors and uptown collectors." Paper Magazine

The Fun Gallery, created by Mudd Club regulars Bill Stelling and Patti Astor, was the first gallery in the then gritty East Village. Whilst it helped to break new graffiti artists on the scene by giving them one man shows (Basquiat and Kenny Scharf included), Keith had a different motivation. He'd already had his sold out Shafrazi show as well as Documenta 7; he agreed to showing at Fun as a way of supporting the gallery. But, significantly, it was at his show's opening that he first met Andy Warhol. Warhol was already a legend, whose works were uber expensive; he was at Fun to draw energy and 'happeningness' from a new crop of young artists. He invited Keith up to the Factory and they traded works. Keith picked one of guys fucking, and in return had to give Andy a load of his pieces, to reflect their relative value. Andy and Keith began to spend time together, exchanging ideas. What insights Andy gave Keith are undocumented, nor do we know whether Andy ever suggested a collaboration (he eventually went with Basquiat). It was more that Keith had now also received the approval of the Pope of New York Cool.

WHO?
KEITH WITH ANDY, SHORTLY AFTER THEY MET IN 1983.

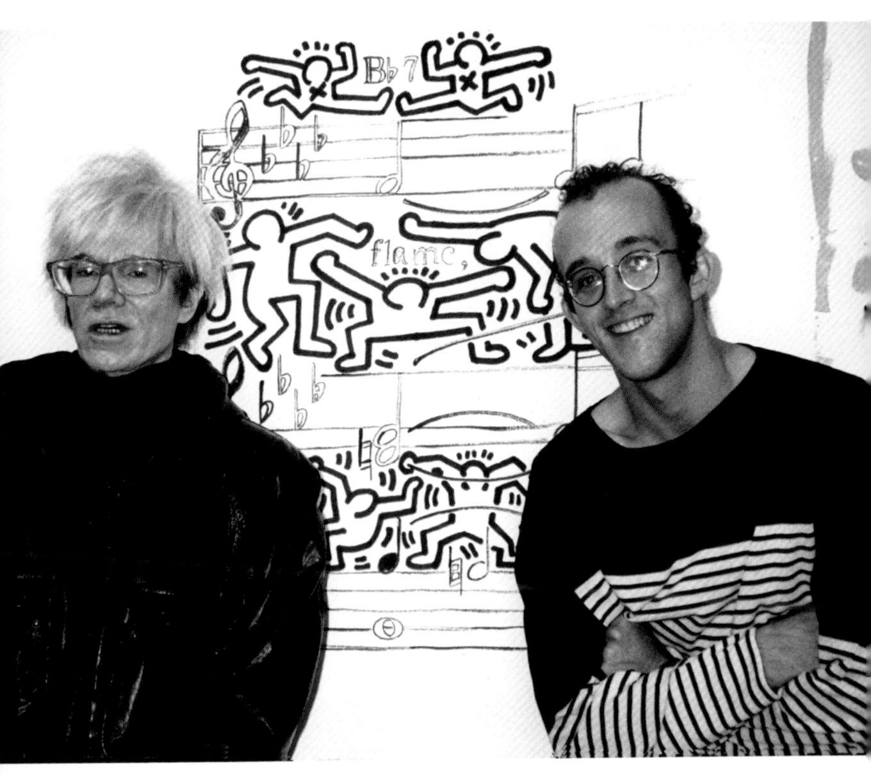
B♭7
flame,

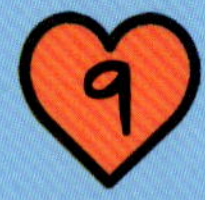

PARADISE GARAGE

"Everyone was there to dance, to sweat, to listen to the music...to get high."

Kat Ayala, dancer

The total antidote to glam Studio 54 uptown, Paradise Garage down in Soho (also known as the 'Gay-rage') was about an amazing sound system, communal dance energy and very short shorts and sneakers. Keith and Jean Dubose both loved to dance – Keith's dancing figures in his artworks were testament to that. It was Fab 5 Freddy who introduced him to Paradise and it was at Paradise that he hung out with Madonna, who performed there before she made it big. Much more than a club to Keith, it became an obsession. He and Jean went there every Saturday night for five years. When he started travelling in Europe, Keith would arrange his itineraries so that he would be back in Soho on a Saturday not to miss the club, flying out again on the Monday if necessary. Larry Levan, the DJ, was known as 'God' or 'The Minister'; the club goers were 'the congregation'. Keith was on a high, living an uncomplicated life, exactly as he wanted it: sex, dancing, drugs and art, with money and recognition flowing easily.

WHERE?
THE PARADISE GARAGE, DANCE AND SWEAT,
SOHO, MANHATTAN.

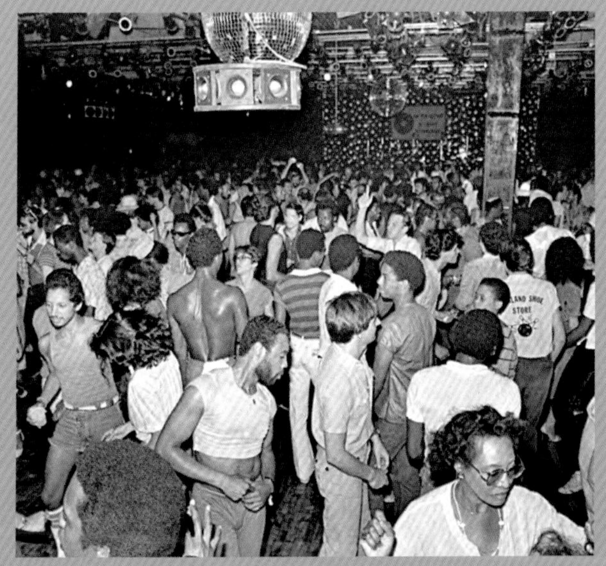

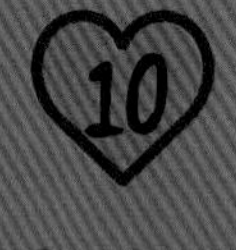

TOKYO

"His vision is...one where everybody could have a piece of the pie." **The New York Times**

Word spread fast about Keith. No sooner had he finished at Documenta 7 than he was invited to show at the Galerie Watari in Tokyo. Keith flew Jean Dubose and LA II out to join him for the opening. It was almost like being back in SVA – rather than ship works out, Keith bought a bunch of materials in Tokyo and then proceeded to create the artworks for the show. That was the thing about Keith – he had an inate feel for line, a simple direct cartoonish idea, all executed really quickly. That graffiti training had been very, very useful. The owners of the gallery, entering into the graffiti spirit, asked Keith to paint the entire facade of the building opposite the gallery. Huge media publicity for the show was the result and the opening was a big success. From having wanted to ignore the gallery system, Keith was finding a brilliantly simple way to work with it – he was probably the first artist not to kowtow to the idea of 'fine/significant' art – whether he painted on inside walls, tarps or on the New York subway, it was the same authentic Keith.

WHERE?
GINZA DISTRICT, TOKYO, IN 1984.

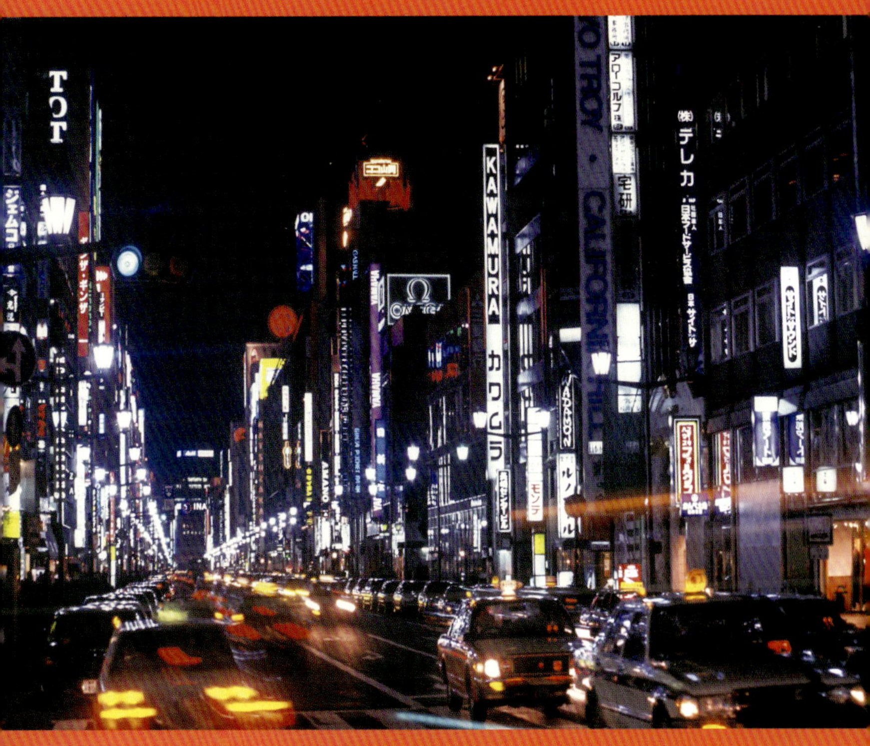
KAWAMURA
カワムラ
(株)
デレカ
ザ・ギンザ
宅研
モンテ

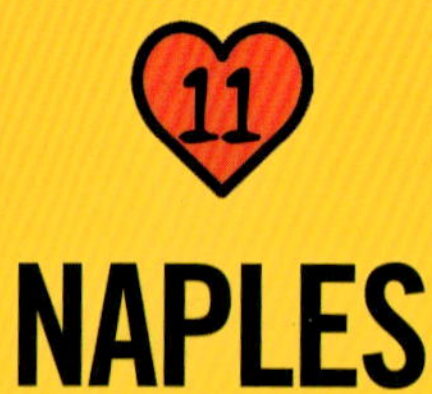

NAPLES

"[My work]...had already spread throughout the world...[on]...T-shirts...in Japan... sneakers in Brazil...dresses in Australia..."

Keith

It all kept flowing, and in between Keith was making sure that he was back at the Paradise Garage every weekend. After Tokyo, in was Naples, specifically the Lucio Amelio gallery, calling. If anything, Italian art dealers had been far more astute at supporting the avant garde than NYC dealers. They had been early supporters of Warhol and Basquiat and now turned to Keith as the next new big thing. Like Tokyo, Keith created original shows on-site and took it a stage further by coming up with the simple, brilliant idea of painting a naked student with his hieroglyphics and lines. This was intended initially for publicity, but was soon to be repeated to brilliant effect as another side to Haring's work. By painting on the naked form, the almost primeval nature of Haring's art came to life, and echoed African body decoration. It was all very new, very fun, very exciting. The pictures were printed in Rome's very hip, counter-cultural *Frigidaire* magazine, to great acclaim. At this point, no one was more hip than Keith.

WHERE?
VIEW OF NAPLES, WITH MOUNT VESUVIUS IN THE DISTANCE.

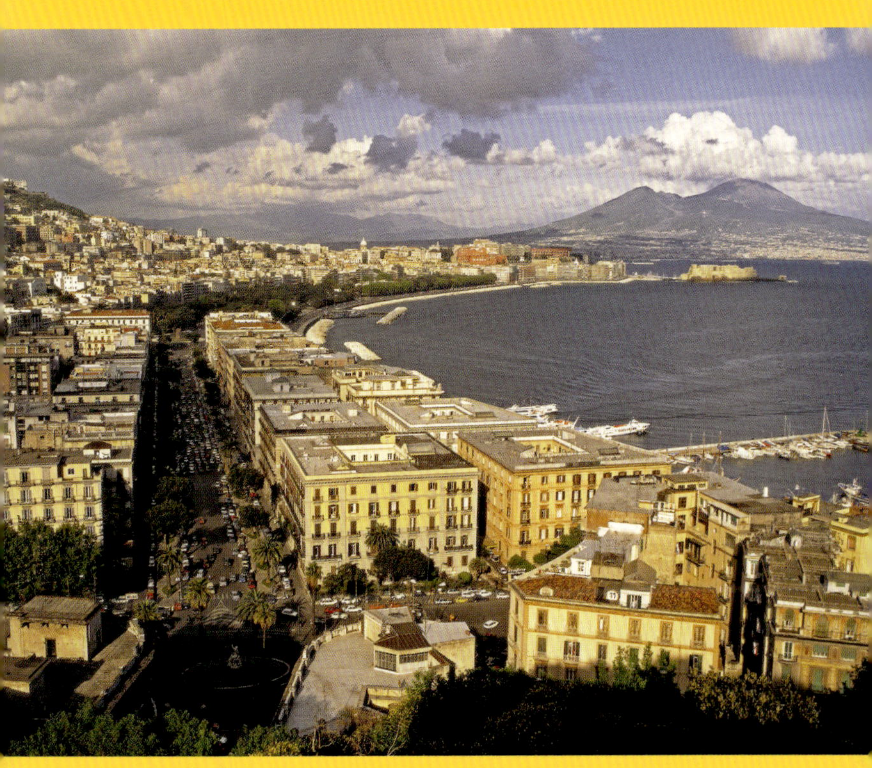

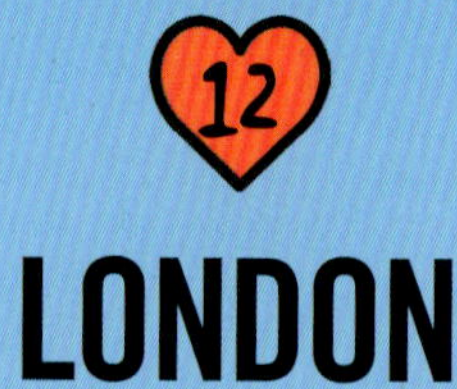

LONDON

***"I really loved the fact that he was a tag artist..."* Bill T. Jones**

Dance choreographer, and Tony Award winning dancer, Bill T. Jones, who revolutionised modern dance with his Jones/ Zane troupe, was in London when Keith asked him if he'd like to be the subject of his latest body painting, to coincide with the opening of Haring's first London show at Robert 'Groovy Bob' Fraser's gallery in Cork Street. Bill, who knew Keith from Kutztown days, readily agreed, not least as a way of promoting his dance work. Keith created these astonishing patterns all over Bill's magnificent dancer's body, from head to toe, including three rings around his penis – a moment that Bill described as "total communion". Kwong Chi photographed the four hour session. London was another triumph for Keith – he collaborated with Malcolm McLaren and Vivienne Westwood, who featured his barking dogs and crawling babies in her 1983 Autumn/ Winter collection. The fashion and music set loved Keith's work – he would go on to create album covers for David Bowie and Run DMC.

WHO?
WORK IN PROGRESS: KEITH PAINTING THE ELEGANT BILL T. JONES IN LONDON, 1983.

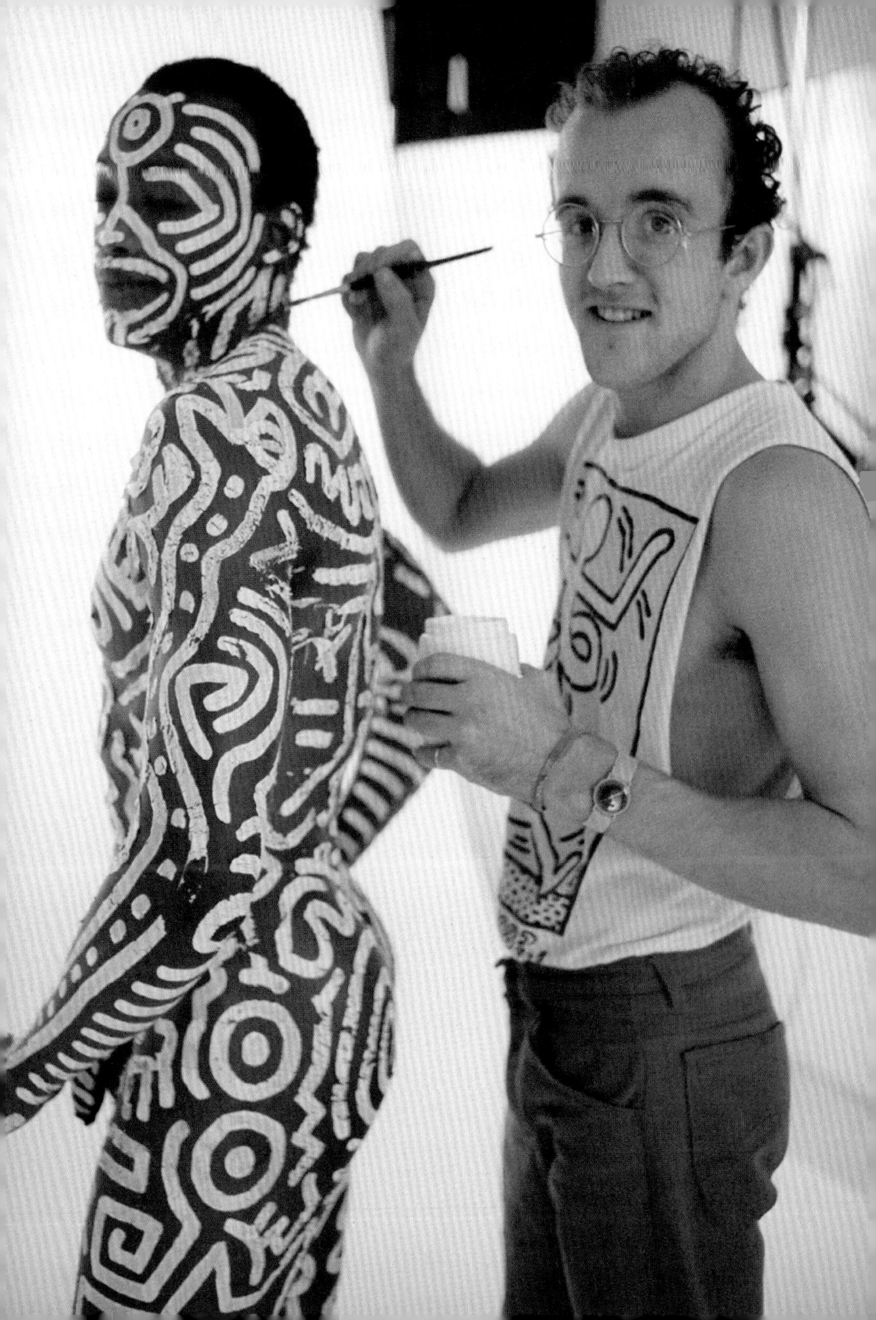

SUCCESS IN THE SHADOW OF AIDS

At first it was sinister, but not too alarming. There was also very, very little information about this new syndrome, initially named, in 1981, GRID – 'Gay-Related Immune Deficiency', which had affected a tiny number of people. Very quickly experts in the field realised that other groups, such as intravenous drug users and haemophiliacs, were also showing symptoms. This was not, as politicians would have it, a 'gay plague', but it began to affect the gay community disproportionately. Keith first mentioned it in his writings in 1982; his first acquaintance to die from the effects of AIDS/HIV was Klaus Nomi in 1983. And then the toll started rising steadily. His reaction, and that of many others, was to be mindful, to carry on having lots of sex, but *safe* sex. As far as his career went, it became even more turbocharged. Sure, he recognised that by 1985, the increasing death toll amongst the creative community from AIDS had changed New York, but it had not yet changed Keith. For him, these were fantastically productive years on an international level – in Europe and Japan as well as the US. Keith had all sorts of new directions going on – his amazing AIDS activism was to come later.

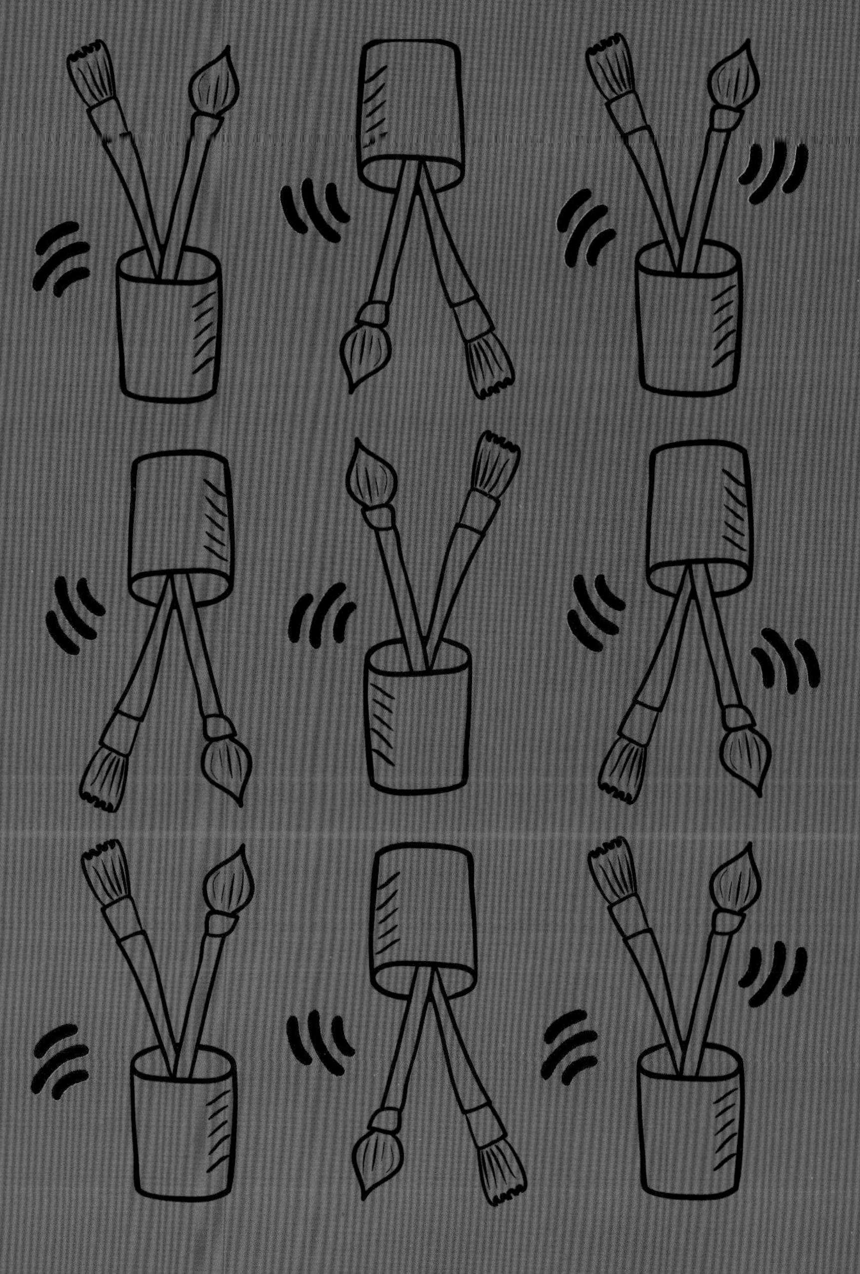

TONY SHAFRAZI 3

"One of the foremost achievements of an artist is to push forward the idea of what can be considered art." **Jeffrey Deitch**

Tony Shafrazi, who had been in London with Keith and had seen his media impact there, wasted little time when they were back in New York mounting Keith's second show. This time as well as the Soho gallery space he hired a big space around the corner on Houston Street. The upstairs was painted by Keith in dayglo colours, whilst the downstairs was turned into a breakdance club, with Jean Dubose as DJ. The club ran every night for a whole month. For the show Keith featured blown-up photos of the Bill T. Jones body art and some new wood pieces. Now instead of painting his lines, he mastered a router and sank the lines in grooves, painting them with dayglo, creating an amazing 3-D effect. Keith was effectively proving that this visual language – that amazing sense of free line with its cartoonish, refreshingly childish feel, had no bounds: drawings, paintings, tarps, walls, amazing naked bodies, wood – he could subsume them all.

WHO?
KEITH IN 1984, AT THE TIME OF HIS SECOND SHAFRAZI SHOW.

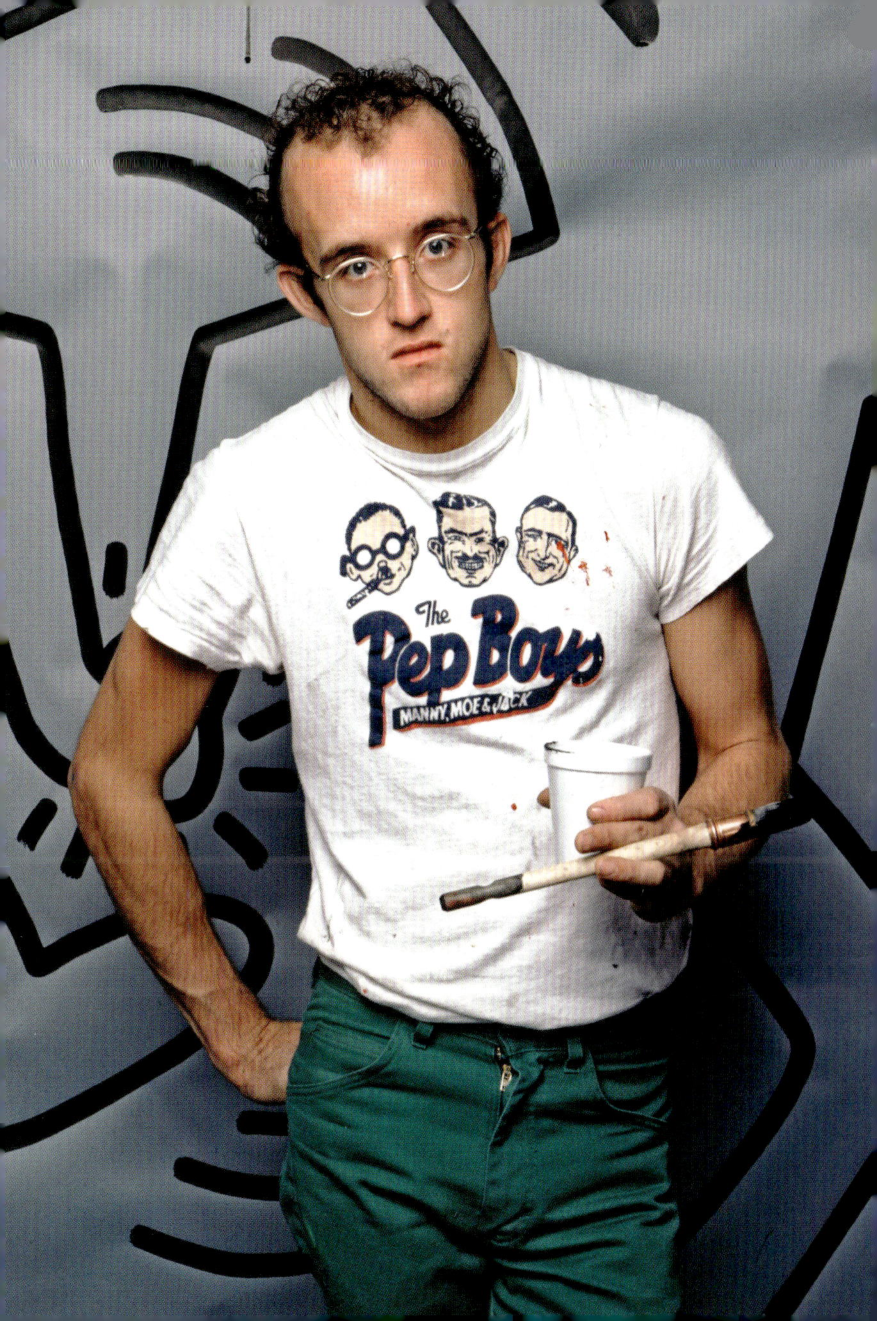
The
Pep Boys
MANNY, MOE & JACK

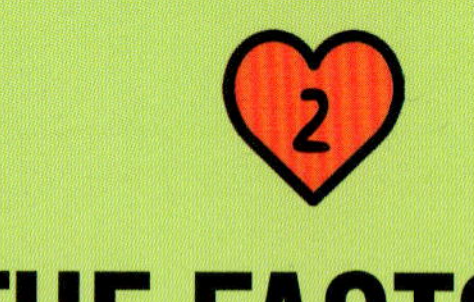

THE FACTORY

"Andy is like a magnet."

Keith Haring

Andy Warhol had turned up at Keith's second show at Shafrazi, then after Iowa City, Andy invited him to come and hang at The Factory. Keith loved the attention he received there and the fact that The Factory was seemingly a meeting place for every celebrity and wealthy collector in Manhattan. According to Paige Powell, Andy's assistant, Keith was pretty open about loving being close to fame. She was handling the advertising/ publicity side of *Interview* magazine and had been responsible for other commercial commissions. Absolute Vodka had asked Andy to design a label for them and it was Andy in turn who suggested Keith as a possible next artist. Of the many artists who designed labels, Haring's design was the most succesful. The Factory was to lead Keith to another of his most striking works – the result of Andy introducing him to Grace Jones.

WHO?
ANDY AND KEITH HANGING OUT IN 1984.

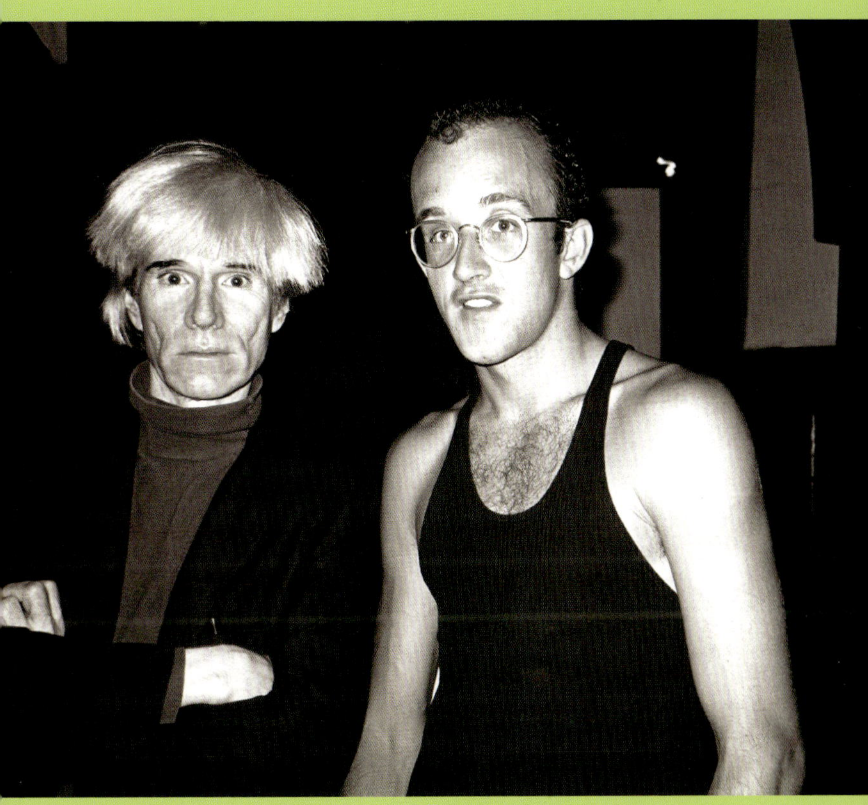

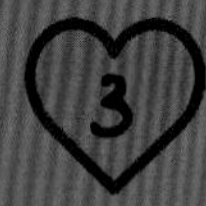

GRACE JONES

"Keith Haring and Grace Jones...created nothing less than pure artistic magic."

Art-Sheep Blog

It all started off being Andy's idea. What if he painted Grace Jones's amazing body in the same way that he had Bill T. Jones, but they got Robert Mapplethorpe to photograph the session? They headed over to Mapplethorpe's studio and Keith set to work, with Jones just wearing bikini bottoms. He had taken the body painting concept much further, creating a conical wire bra for Jones, amazing white markings all over her and an astonishing headdress several feet tall, with African-looking jewellery hanging provocatively between her legs. According to Keith Grace in this guise was 'the embodiment of everything that's primitive and pop', and his design for her body paint and costume echoed Inuit, African, Mayan and Aboriginal art. The result was one of Keith's most enduring and vibrant creations, and was reused by Grace for the film *Vamp* (1986) and for a huge ballgown (1987). It also had lost none of its vitality nearly 30 years later when Rihanna was inspired by Keith's designs used in the brilliant video for her hit *Rude Boy* (2013).

WHO?
GRACE JONES IN *VAMP*.

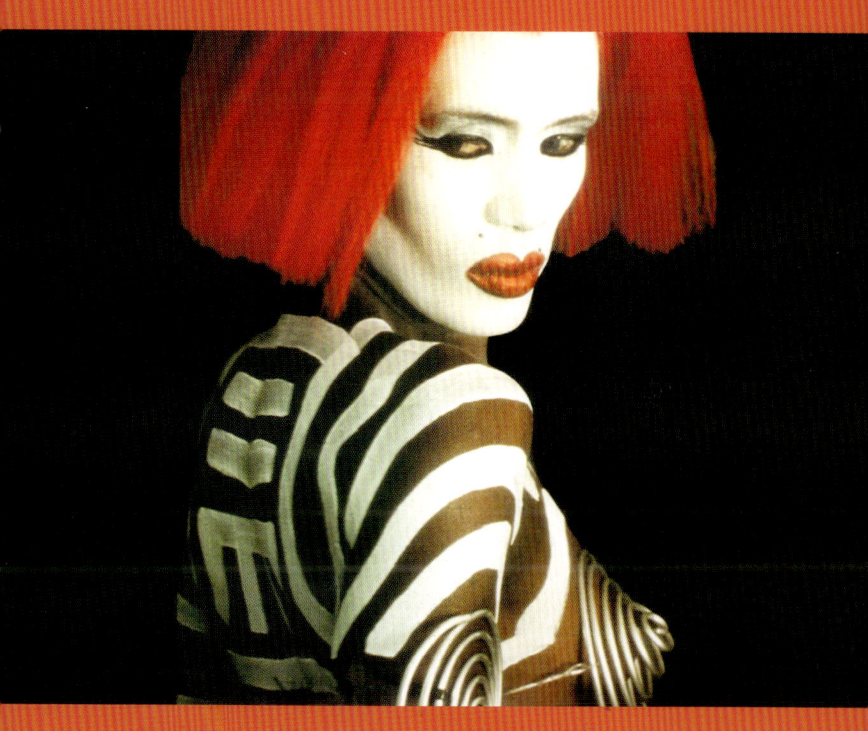

KEITH'S MANHATTAN

Keith arrived in Manhattan in 1979 – the perfect time. The city was dangerous, and in parts really run down with a huge drug problem in Tribeca, the East Village and Soho. This was the perfect environment however for artists and bands to thrive and Keith found himself at the centre of a music, club and art scene bursting with potential. Madonna, Basquiat, Kenny Scharf, Klaus Nomi, John Sex, Debbie Harry and Blondie, Bowie, Steve Rubell, Ian Schrager, Fab 5 Freedy were just a few of the names that Keith was hanging out with. Amazing, given that Keith was just a boy from Kutztown.

❶ Paradise Garage
84 King Street, Hudson Square.
The edgiest, most happening dance club in Manhattan. The DJ was amazing, the vibe was very gay with a strong African-American contingent. This was the one place that Keith felt 100% at home.

❷ The Palladium
126 East 14th Street.
Steve Rubell's mega club after Studio 54 was shut by the IRS. This was an uptown scene for the beautiful people. Keith had created the central dancefloor artwork. The club also had works by Basquiat and Scharf.

❸ Studio
676 Broadway, Broadway and West 3rd.
Keith's last studio before his death. It was a huge space and round the corner from his last apartment.

❹ Pop Shop
292 Lafayette Street, Soho.
Keith's brilliant retail outlet became a cult go-to shop, allowing Keith to merchandise his brilliant imagery. It stayed open until 2005.

❺ Crack is Wack
East Harlem Drive, 128th Street.
The location of Keith's anti-Crack billboard, which he painted on impulse in 1986. It has been restored many times.

❻ The Mudd Club
77 White Street, Tribeca.
Steve Mass's brilliant club in druggy and dangerous Tribeca became the centre of possibly the most creative scene in Manhattan. Keith also curated artshows here, bringing Uptown graffiti artists downtown for the first time. Soon Warhol, Bowie, Bianca Jagger and Yoko Ono also became regulars.

❼ Danceteria
West 37th and 8th Avenue.
Brilliant dance club where Madonna first performed before she made it. Keith was a busboy here for a while.

❽ Tony Shafrazi Gallery
163 Mercer Street, Soho.
Keith got his first exposure to the NYC artworld here, working as Tony's assistant. During his life, Keith held two major solo shows at the Shafrazi Gallery, in 1982 and 1984.

❾ Leo Castelli Gallery
142 Greene Street, Soho.
It was probably Tony Shafrazi who suggested sculpture to Keith, but with his blessing the solo show was held at uber-dealer, Leo Castelli's gallery.

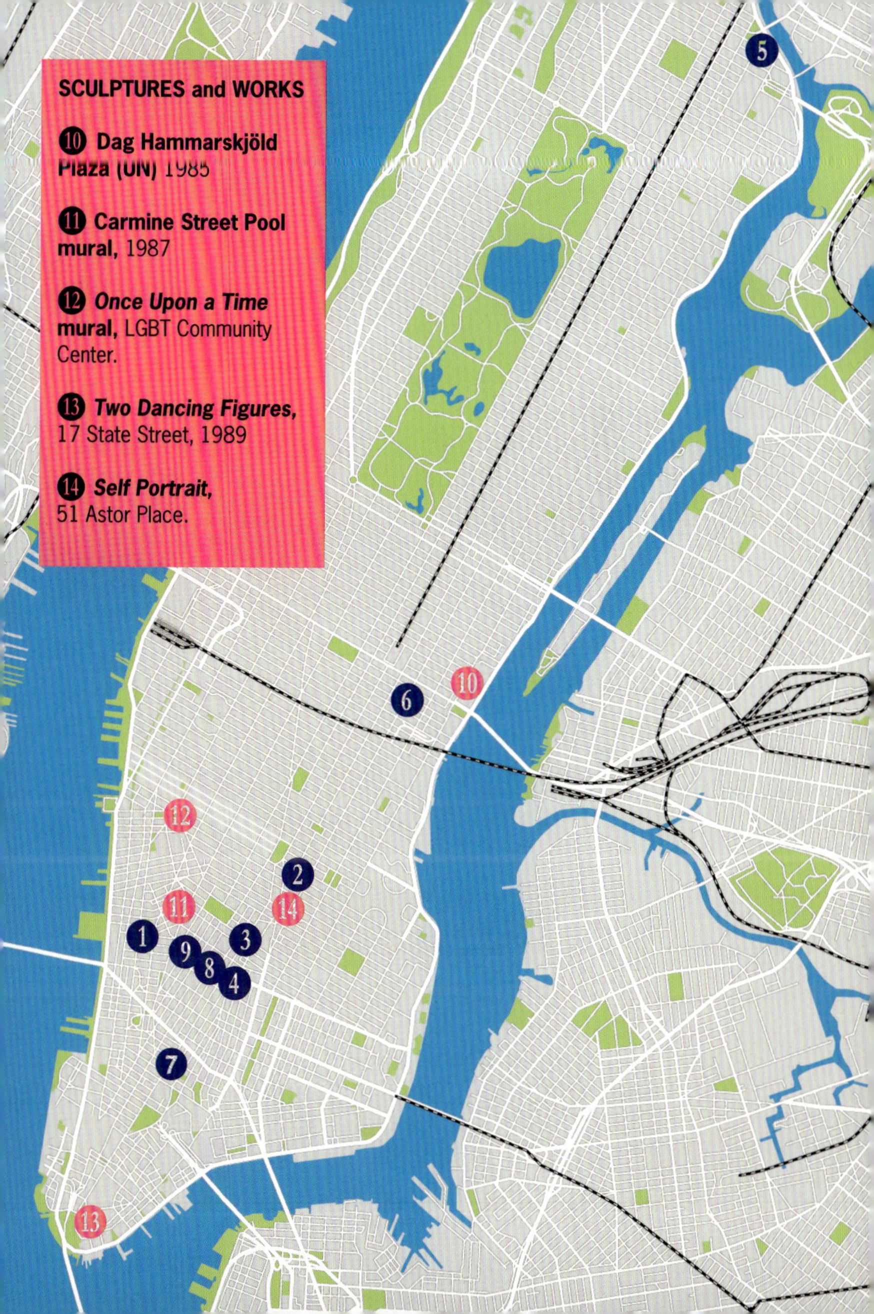
SCULPTURES and WORKS
10 Dag Hammarskjöld Plaza (UN) 1985
11 Carmine Street Pool mural, 1987
12 Once Upon a Time mural, LGBT Community Center.
13 Two Dancing Figures, 17 State Street, 1989
14 Self Portrait, 51 Astor Place.
1
2
3
4
5
6
7
8
9
10
11
12
13
14

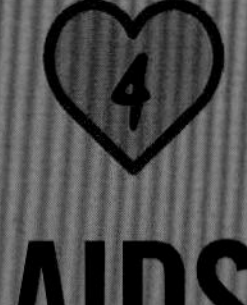

AIDS

"It was a terrifying time...[AIDS] was a catastrophe, invisible to so many people."
Andrew Sullivan

The first AIDS cases in New York had been identified in 1981. At the time there was little understanding of the disease – because gay men were the first to be diagnosed, it became tagged as a 'gay plague' or 'gay cancer' and the right-wing Reagan and Ed Koch (mayor, NYC) establishments at the time used its emergence as a way of heaping moral opprobium on a community they disapproved of. Keith first mentioned it in his writings in 1982. The carefree, fun years of going to the bath houses for anonymous sex were over. The first person Keith knew to die from AIDS was Klaus Nomi, the singer, who succumbed in 1983. Keith now became more selective about his partners and practiced safe sex. In his writings, he only began to say how much it was changing New York in 1985. But his energy was irrepressible and he wasn't at this point going to let a fear of AIDS get in the way of his art or playful spirit. Two years later, with many more friends succumbing, AIDS was to become central to Keith's life.

WHAT?
NYC AIDS POSTER BY ACT-UP, RAISING AWARENESS OF THE DISEASE IN THE FACE OF US GOVERNMENT INACTION.

SILENCE = DEATH

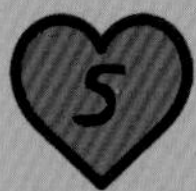

LEO CASTELLI GALLERY

"We Americans are...influenced by a cartoon culture. That's why Keith Haring is so important." **Leo Castelli**

It was Tony Shafrazi who came up with the suggestion that Keith should turn his attention to outdoor sculpture. The strength of Keith's very simple aesthetic was that it could easily be transferred into striking metal shapes. He had a ready made cast of characters – his dogs, babies and child shapes. Painting them in bright colours would look great against glass skyscrapers. Leo Castelli – New York's most powerful dealer now came on board. He would hold a show of Keith's sculptures, whilst Shafrazi would show new 2-D work. Keith could do no wrong. The Castelli show was a triumph and three of his pieces were chosen for the Plaza in front of the UN building. The childish, cartoonish optimism and exuberance of Keith's work struck a chord of energised fun, suggesting also that the UN's work should be about a better future for children. Castelli explained it all simply – Americans are influenced by cartoon culture, which is why Haring spoke to them so directly. Keith, still only 27, was now one of the most famous artists in the US.

WHERE?
NYC'S MOST POWERFUL DEALER, LEO CASTELLI, MIXED IT WITH HIGH SOCIETY, SEEN HERE WITH LIZ TAYLOR.

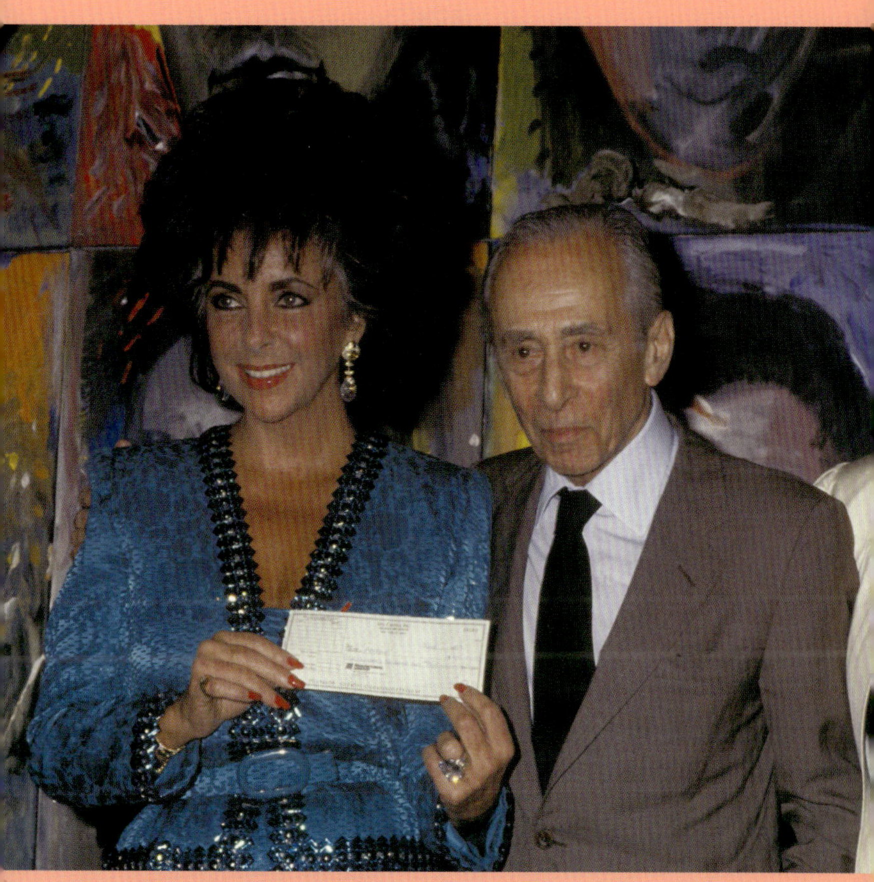

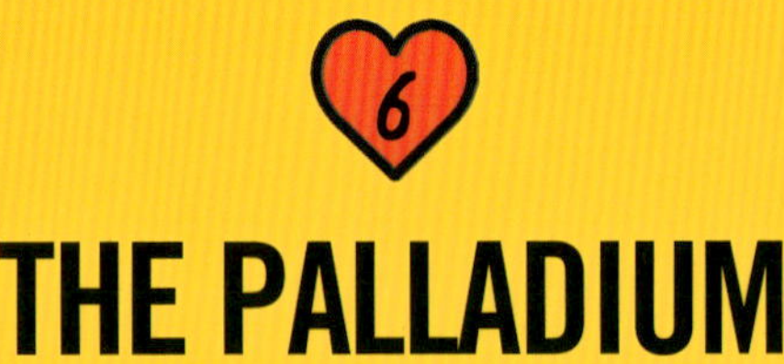

THE PALLADIUM

***"A creative hub for more than just visual artists: New wave, house and techno blossomed here..."* The New York Times**

When Steve Rubell, one of the former owners of legendary Studio 54, got out of jail for tax fraud in 1981 he decided to repeat the success of '54 with a new mega club – The Palladium. Rubell hired Japanese architect Arata Isozaki to convert the space and commissioned several mega artists – Basquiat and Clemente in addition to Haring – to create original artworks. Keith's painting – a huge backdrop to the main dance floor had pride of place. It was a statement of his cool celebrity artist status, not just in the New York art world, but amongst New York glitterati. Keith held a huge 'Party of Life' there when it finally opened in 1985, inviting 5000 people, all of whom got a Haring T-shirt. As usual it was a riot of celebrities and attendant wannabes trying to get in. Keith was on a high, but also at home – the lead DJ was Richard Sweret, who had been a DJ at Danceteria. As ever with Keith he was at once existing in a social stratosphere, but also grounded in the very familiar.

WHERE?
KEITH WITH FRIEND, OPENING NIGHT PARTY AT THE PALLADIUM.
140 EAST 14TH STREET,
MANHATTAN.

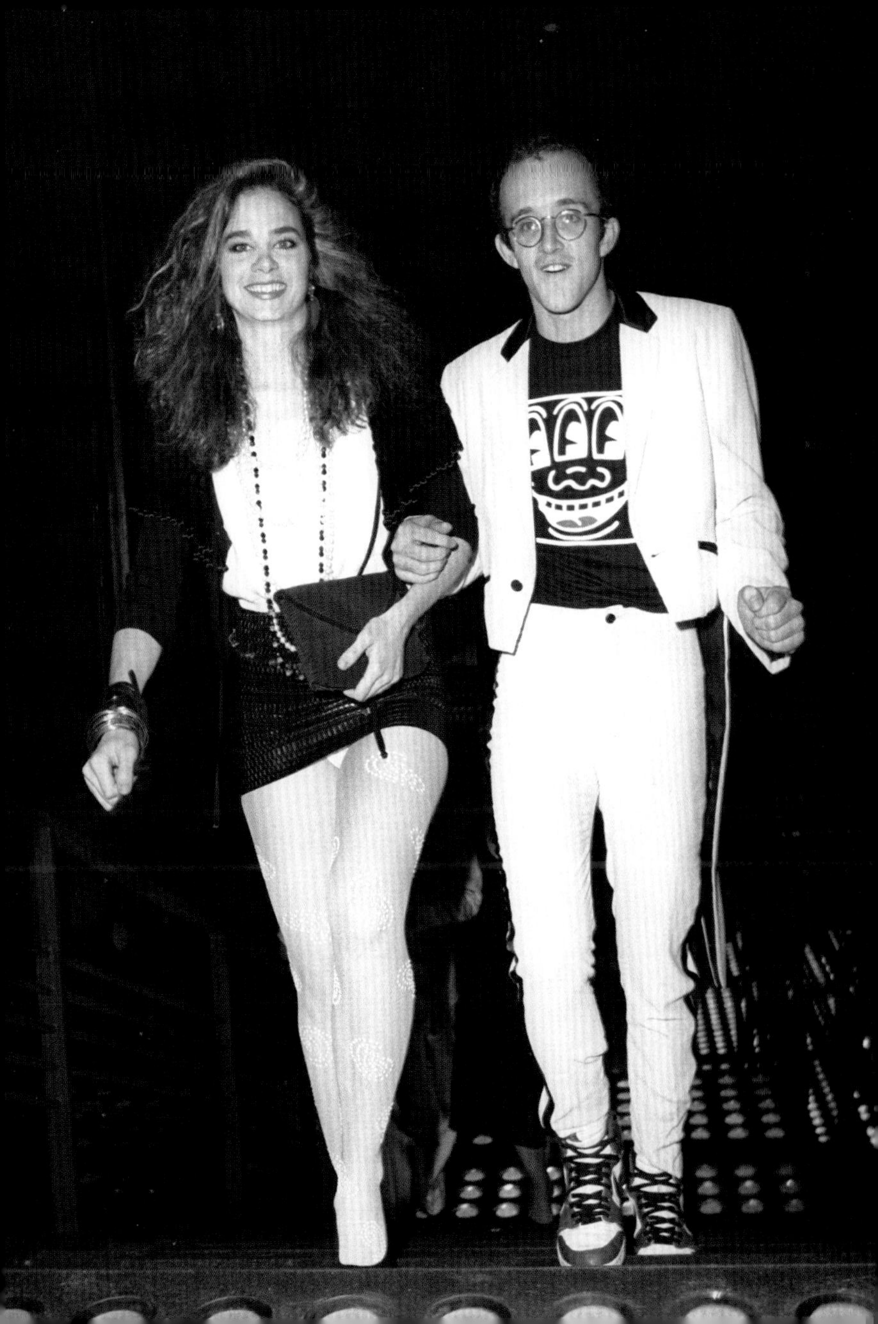

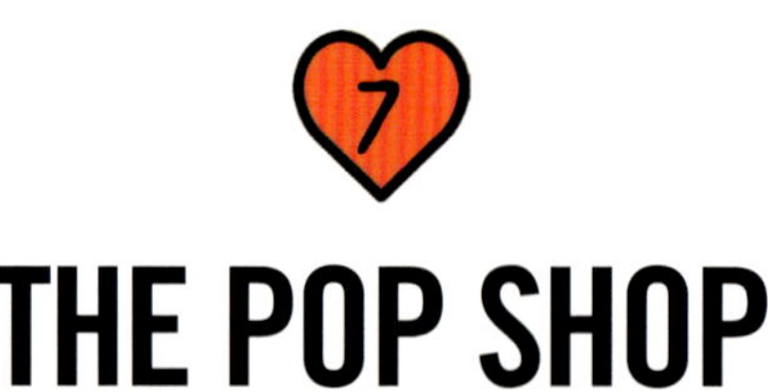

THE POP SHOP

"My shop is... breaking down the barriers between high and low art."

Keith in The New York Times

Keith's art was so original, so recognisably him, that it was eminently merchandisable. He had got this early on when doing the subway drawings. Rather than engage with people (he had no time, had to work superfast) he would hand out button badges with one of his designs. He had also created T-shirt designs and posters of his work. It was a way for Keith to create art for everyone – no gallery barriers, no intimidating 'fine art' definitions. Keith was also easy to copy and he began to see that pirate merchandise was starting to appear. Free-thinking soul that he was, Keith took it to the next level – why not just open a shop for his merchandise and art? As he said at the time, he wanted everyone to be able to buy Haring – including kids from the Bronx. The shop, with ceilings walls and floors painted by Haring in a glossy black and white motif, was both a commercial and artistic statement, stated Keith, when he opened it on Lafayette, with Bobby Breslau as manager. It was an instant hit – school kids would play hooky just to be in time to grab the latest bit of merchandise. It stayed open until 2005.

WHERE?
KEITH AT THE OPENING OF THE POP SHOP, LAFAYETTE STREET, MANHATTAN, 1986.

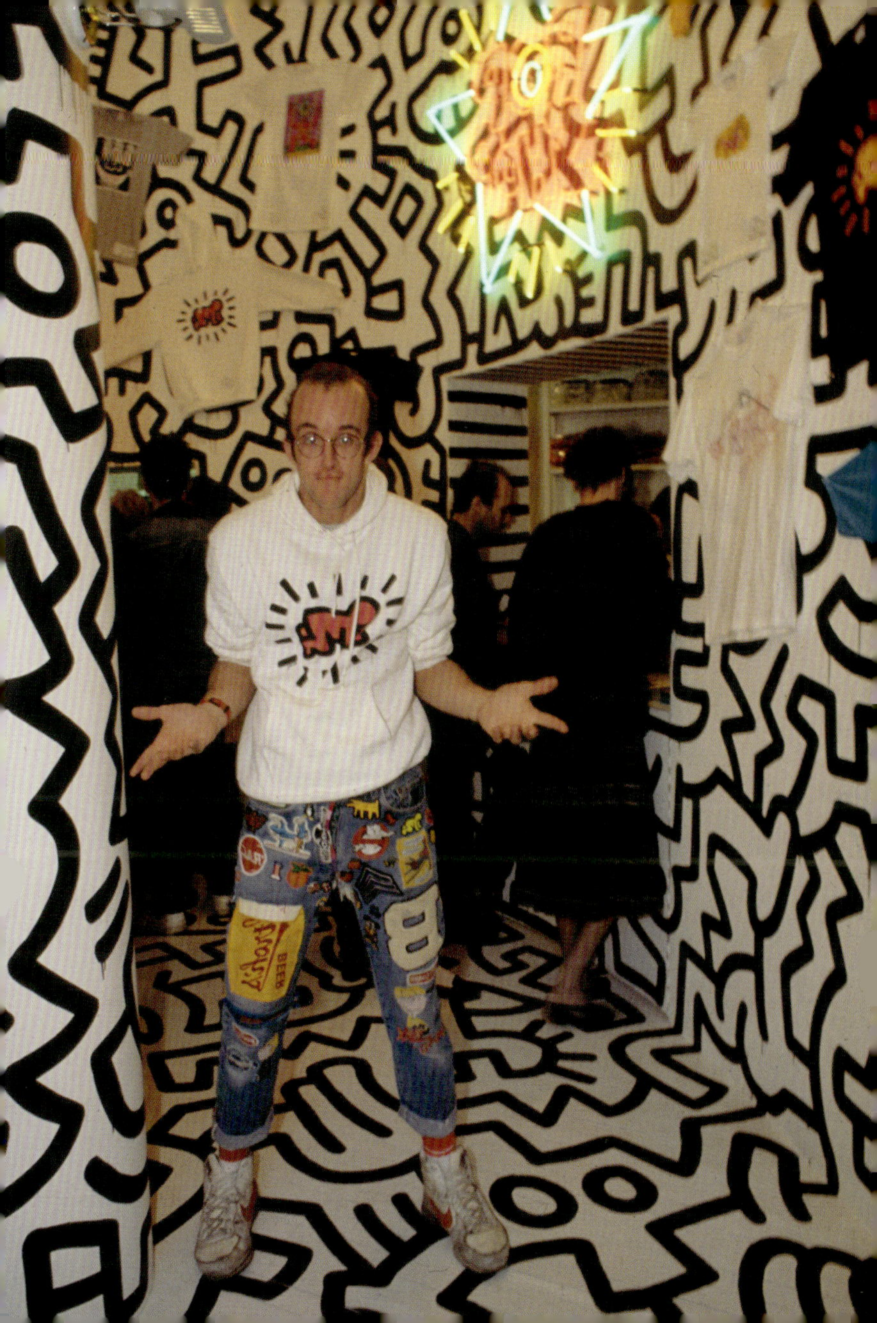

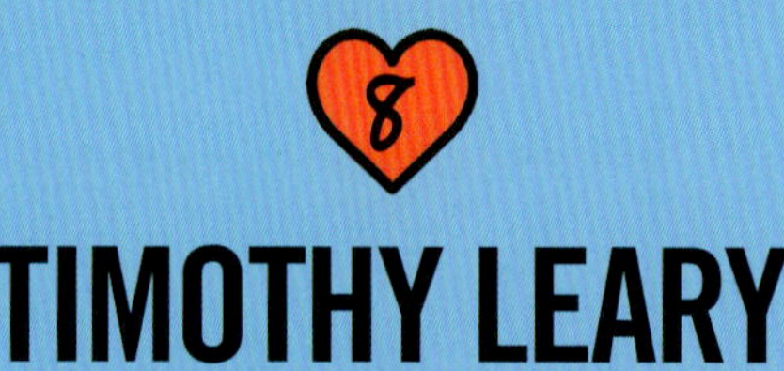

TIMOTHY LEARY

"Your style is, more than any other artist's, geared to 21st century expressions."
Timothy Leary, letter to Keith

Keith had repainted Grace Jones for some stunning performance at the Paradise Garage in 1985. In 1986 he was in Paris painting a 60ft-wide skirt for her video *I'm Not Perfect*. As ever, his trip was arranged so he could be back at Paradise at the weekend. Significantly for Keith, Grace introduced him to the LSD apostle Timothy Leary. They instantly clicked. Haring completely bought into the Leary doctrine of the mind-expanding possibilities of LSD. Leary saw Keith as an artist for the 21st Century – his art instantly and very easily understood by everyone, perfect for the time when so much shared information would lead to a complete breakdown of artificial barriers. Leary was Keith's first proper introduction to the implications of computers. Keith for Leary had that child-like open quality which was, he thought, the future. Prophetic stuff: Keith the artist for the non-serious, playful, hyper-energetic 21st Century. To prove it, Keith contributed art to Leary's visionary *Neuromancer* videogame, sadly never commercially produced.

WHO?
LSD GURU TIMOTHY LEARY ("THE MOST DANGEROUS MAN IN AMERICA", ACCORDING TO RICHARD NIXON), WITH HIS WIFE ROSEMARY.

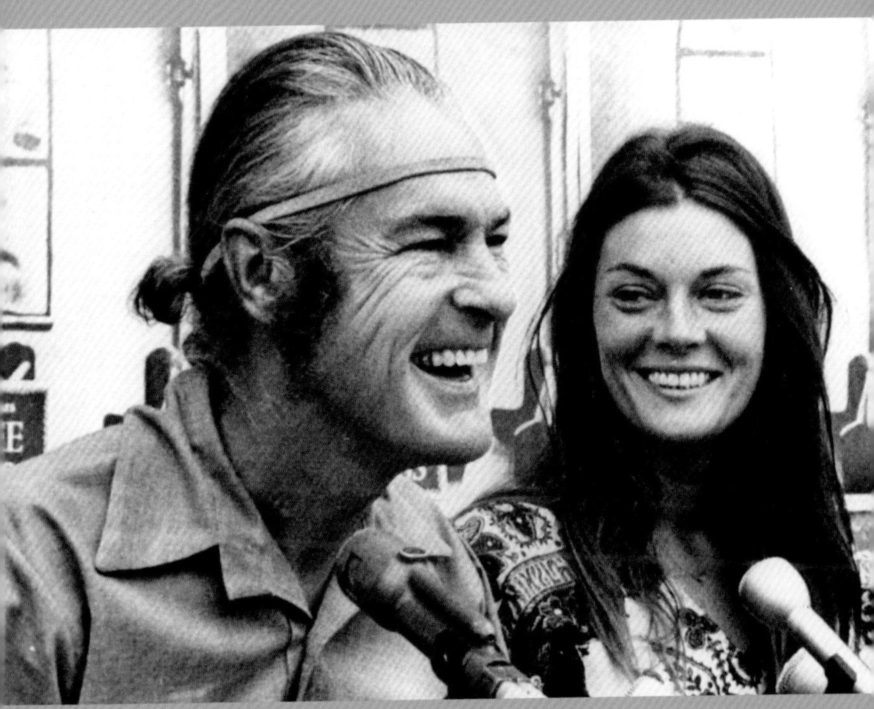

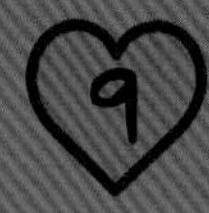

CRACK IS WACK

"It took Keith a day to paint – and about a million hours to practice!"
Louise Hunnicutt, mural restorer

Crack is Wack, a mural painted on a billboard on the approaches to the Triborough Bridge (maximum exposure), was one of Keith's first 'activist' works. As on the subway he didn't ask permission, but got his message up there. Keith was used to experimenting with drugs, but he was careful to control the boundaries, unlike many friends who struggled with addiction. Keith was appalled by government inaction at a crack epidemic which was particularly affecting black communities in Harlem. As Keith was finishing the work, he was approached by NYPD and served with a summons for defacing public property. But Keith had made his point. The work became notorious and got much coverage when crack was discussed in the media. The piece was vandalised by some locals, but then in a delicious irony, the Parks Department Commissioner asked Keith to restore his own 'illegal' work, and it became a local fixture. In 2019, the mural underwent a deep restoration, led by artist Louise Hunnicutt.

WHERE?
EAST HARLEM DRIVE (TRIBOROUGH BRIDGE APPROACHES) BROOKLYN.
KEITH'S MURAL UNDERGOING LOVING RESTORATION IN 2019.

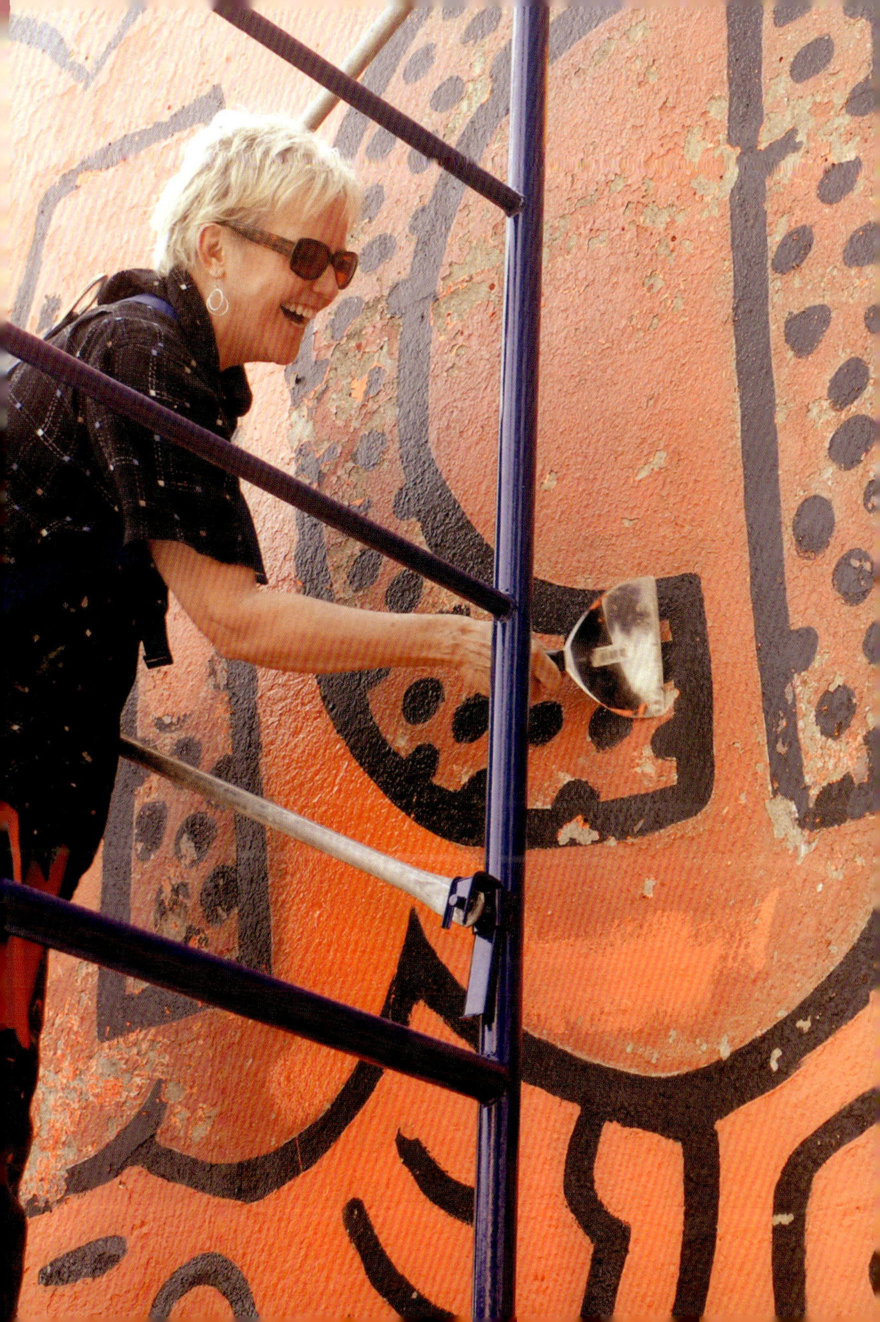

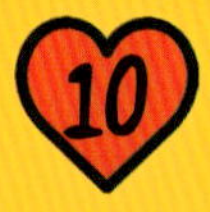

THE BERLIN WALL

"The mural...was as illegal as his original underground graffiti."
The New York Times, report on Keith's Berlin Wall

It was a strange fact that the 6ft of land on the western side of the Berlin Wall in fact belonged to East Germany, so when Keith was invited to paint on the wall by a West German human rights group (which monitored East German abuses), it was a potentially risky undertaking. Keith started work at 10 am, using the colours of the German flag. West German megaphones warned him that he was entering East Germany without a visa. The world's media recorded the event. Armed East German guards kept an eye. Keith said that he wanted to psychologically destroy the wall by painting it, but that it wasn't aimed against East Germany: "It's for people and it doesn't matter which side of the wall they're on. It's about sides coming together," he told *The Times*, a little faux-naively perhaps. The East Germans weren't so keen on the idea. Around 140 people were killed trying to cross from east to west from 1961 when the wall was built, until 1989 when it began to be demolished. Four of those deaths occurred after Keith had painted it.

WHERE?
THE BERLIN WALL. KEITH WORKING ON HIS MURAL WITH ARMED GDR GUARDS KEEPING A CLOSE EYE. WEST BERLIN, WEST GERMANY.

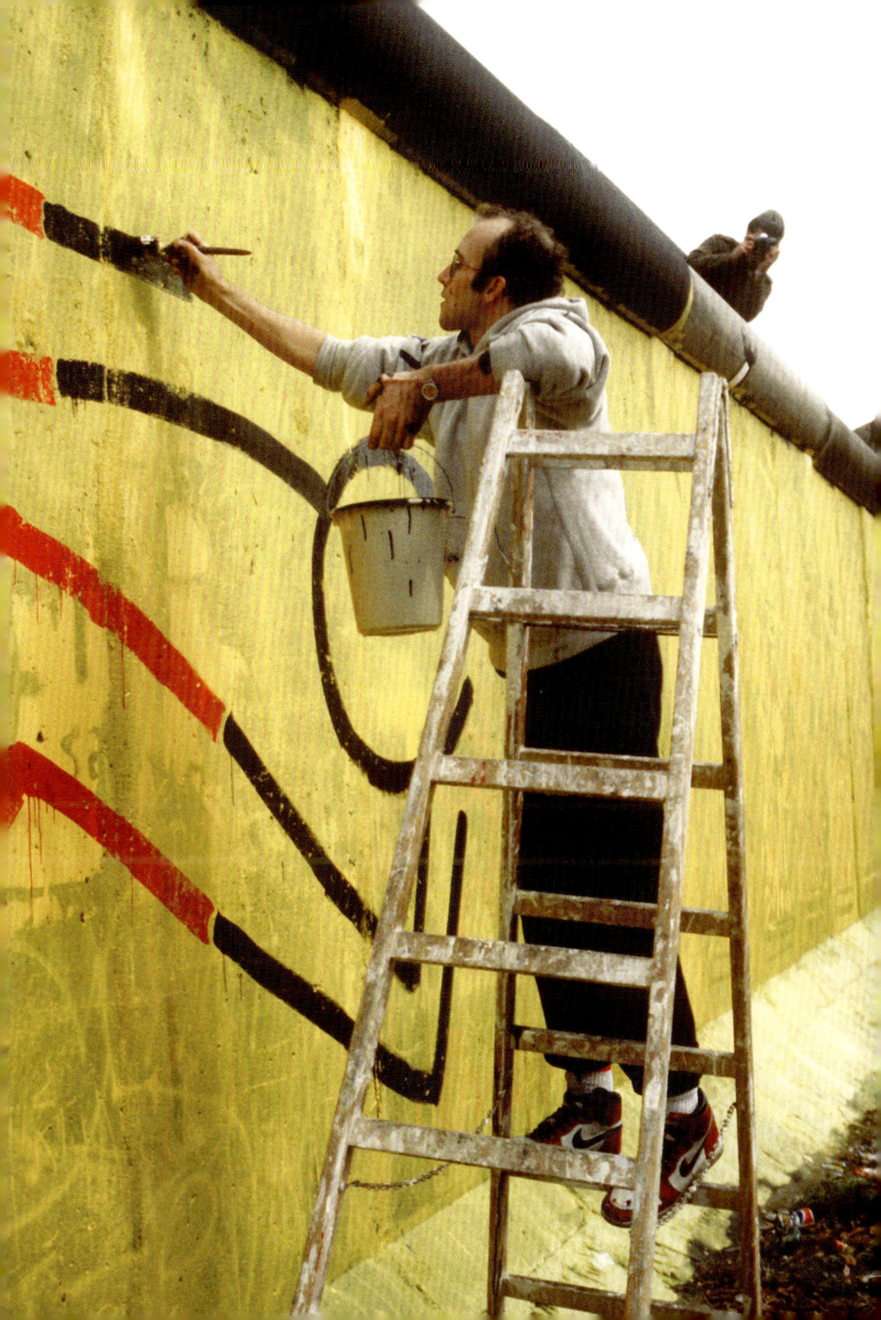

KEITH TRAVELS AND SHOWS 1985-1986

With international success came huge amounts of travel. Keith was now in demand all over the world. He had a massive solo show in Bordeaux, which then travelled to the prestigious Stedelijk in Amsterdam. In New York he was as busy as ever, with two solo shows and his Pop Shop. The 1986 Montreux Festival invited him to create their poster together with Andy Warhol and then Berlin invited him to paint on the Berlin Wall. He had a show in Paris and then holidayed with Kenny Scharf in Brazil. And between these assignments, he would shuttle back so he could be at Paradise Garage every Saturday. Keith travelled on adrenaline: there was little time for jetlag.

NEW YORK

1985: shows at Shafrazi Gallery and Leo Castelli and creates his Palladium installation. 1986: Keith opens the Pop Shop and paints *Crack is Whack* mural. Grace Jones introduces Keith to Timothy Leary.

LOS ANGELES

1986: Keith visits Leary in Beverly Hills, where they discuss the 21st Century and, prophetically, Leary's belief that computers will be ubiquitous.

MINAS GERAIS, BRAZIL

1985-1986: Kenny Scharf and his wife invited Keith a few times to their holiday home in Minas Gerais. Keith loved to visit, but Kenny did not enjoy the company of Keith's boyfriends and invitations later dried up.

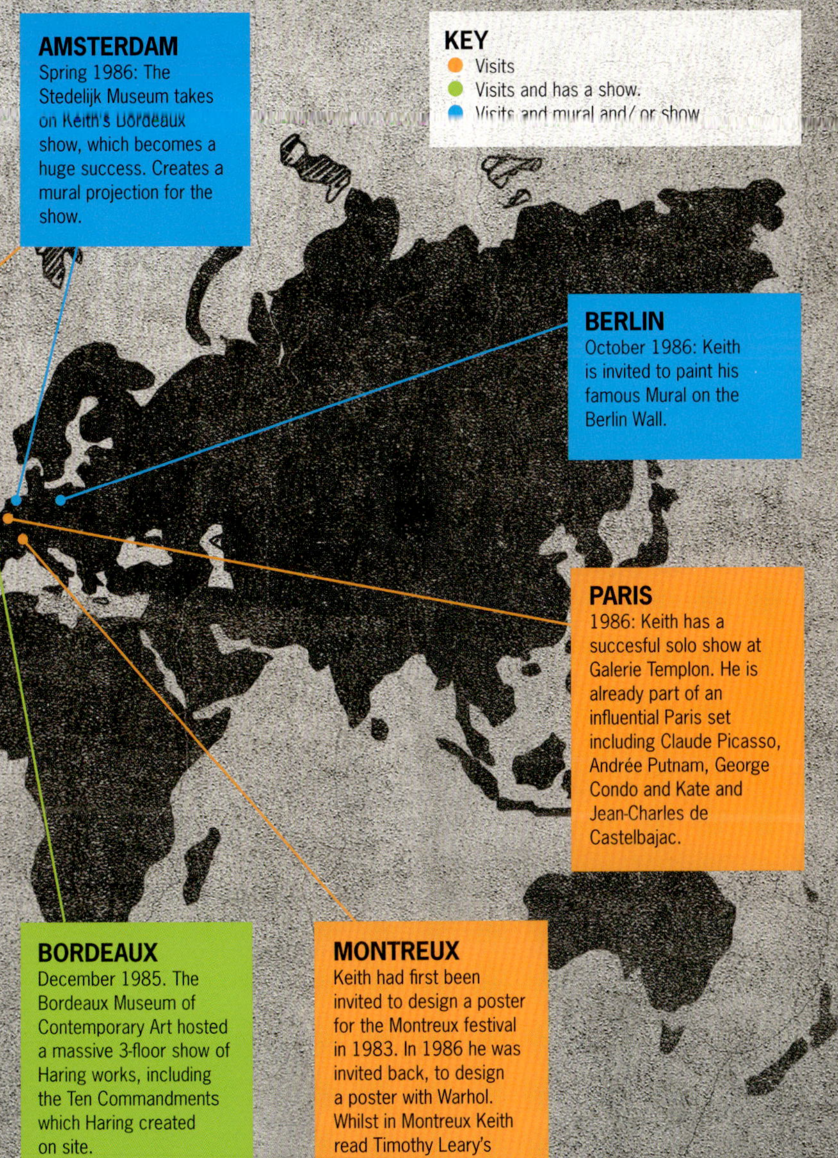
AMSTERDAM
Spring 1986: The Stedelijk Museum takes on Keith's Bordeaux show, which becomes a huge success. Creates a mural projection for the show.
KEY
Visits
Visits and has a show.
Visits and mural and/ or show
BERLIN
October 1986: Keith is invited to paint his famous Mural on the Berlin Wall.
PARIS
1986: Keith has a succesful solo show at Galerie Templon. He is already part of an influential Paris set including Claude Picasso, Andrée Putnam, George Condo and Kate and Jean-Charles de Castelbajac.
BORDEAUX
December 1985. The Bordeaux Museum of Contemporary Art hosted a massive 3-floor show of Haring works, including the Ten Commandments which Haring created on site.
MONTREUX
Keith had first been invited to design a poster for the Montreux festival in 1983. In 1986 he was invited back, to design a poster with Warhol. Whilst in Montreux Keith read Timothy Leary's Flashback.

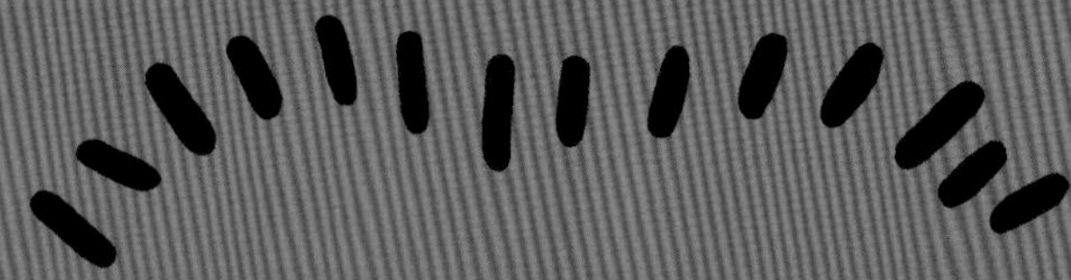

WORKING IN DEATH'S SHADOW

1986 had been such a great year. But then in 1987 everything seemed to change. Bobby Breslau, manager of the Pop Shop, died from AIDS-related complications. Within a month Andy Warhol died following a gall bladder operation. Keith's ex-lover Jean Dubose was diagnosed with AIDS. To cap it all, in Jean-Michel Basquiat then died from an OD, a '88. The number of deaths of AIDS-related conditions in New York was also climbing steeply. Keith knew that he too was probably at risk: it was hard to escape the feeling that death was also stalking him. His response was to throw himself more than ever into his art. As part of this he began his series of works designed to raise awareness of the growing AIDS epidemic. From a quite cheery work of 1988 promoting Safe Sex, his message a year later was far, far more direct: "IGNORANCE = FEAR; SILENCE = DEATH; FIGHT AIDS, ACT UP." For Keith this was now very personal – he was diagnosed as suffering from Kaposi's sarcoma, an AIDS-related cancer, in late 1988. Far from retiring, Keith's reaction was to work harder than ever.

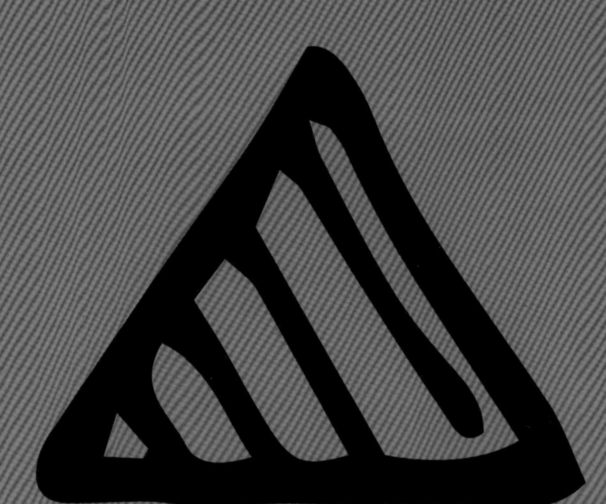

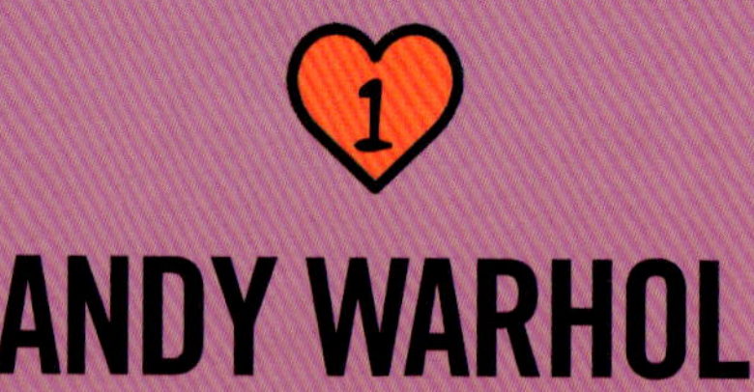

ANDY WARHOL

"It's difficult to imagine New York City without him."
Keith, on the death of Andy.

Keith was in Brazil on holiday when he heard that Andy Warhol had died from complications following a routine gall bladder operation. As for many associated with the Factory, it was a total shock. According to Keith, Andy had achieved the breakthrough in art which had made the whole of Keith's life possible. Without Andy shifting the goalposts of what art meant, Keith could just have ended up as a good graphic commercial artist or cartoonist, living a suburban existence. With Andy's death Keith decided to take a long, three month trip to Europe. He was no longer flying back every weekend to be at Paradise Garage. An imperceptible shift had taken place in Keith's life; he still held onto the childish joy in his imagery, but somehow there was a more serious timbre to his take on life, and soon, death.

WHO?
ANDY WARHOL AND BASQUIAT AT THE OPENING OF THEIR JOINT SHOW AT THE SHAFRAZI GALLERY. THE SUDDEN DEATH OF ANDY IN 1987 CAME AS A TOTAL SHOCK. BASQUIAT WAS DEAD A YEAR LATER, FROM A HEROIN COCKTAIL OVERDOSE.

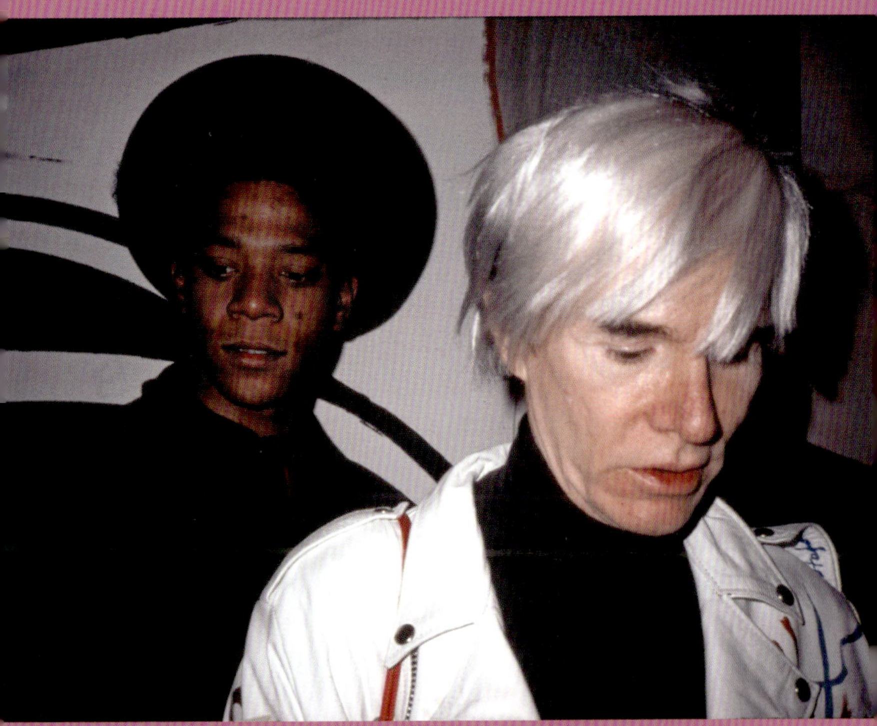

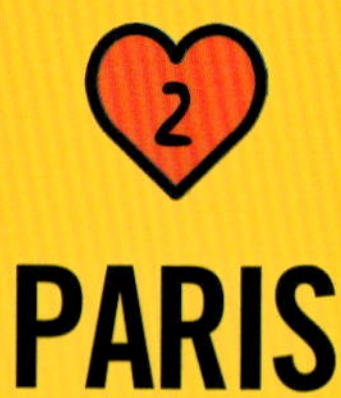

PARIS

***"He had a spot in his heart for Paris throughout his life."* HamiltonSelway.com**

In 1987 the Pompidou Centre in Paris hosted a mega exhibition of the major international artists of the previous decade. Haring was invited to exhibit, together with such luminaries as de Kooning, Dubuffet, Stella, Donald Judd and Anselm Kiefer. Whilst in Paris, Keith painted a large mural at the paediatric Necker hospital, showing his sense of fun and his care for children, uplifting their spirits. (Keith loved the fact that his art was instantly 'got' by children). Keith, who also had a solo show at the Daniel Templon Gallery, was feted and slid easily into the upper echelons of Parisian society, hanging out with the Marquis and Marquise de Castelbajac, Claude and Sydney Picasso, Yoko Ono, US artist George Condo and the mega designer Andrée Putman. Keith was existing happily on his plateau of international mega-success.

WHERE?
KEITH PAINTING A POT, IN THE CASTELBAJAC APARTMENT IN PARIS, WITH JEAN-CHARLES DE CASTELBAJAC LOOKING ON.

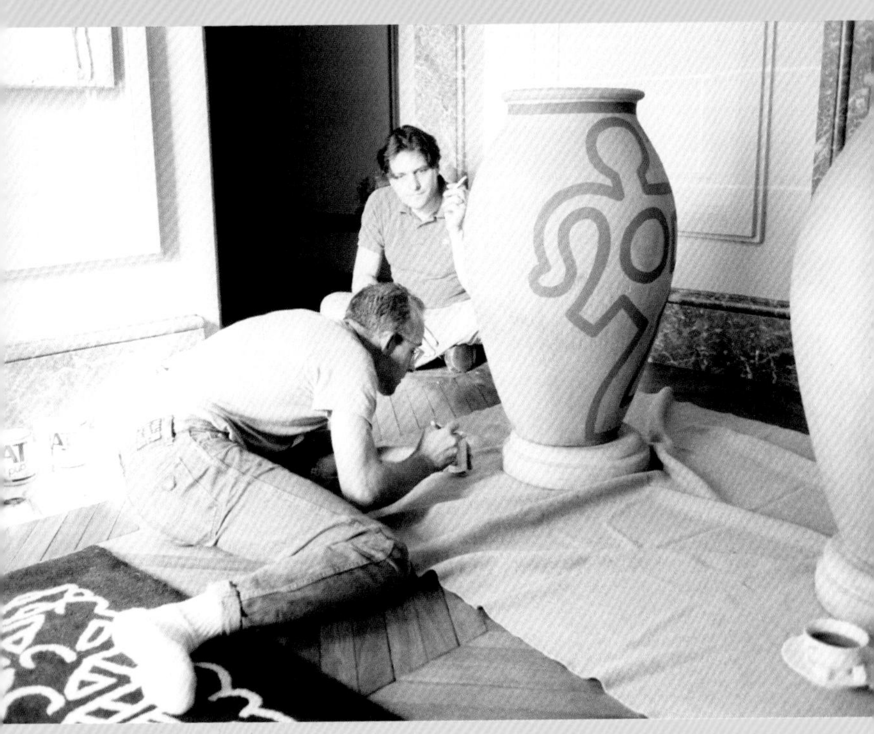

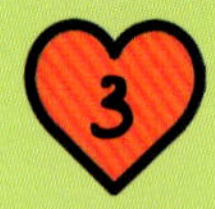

KNOKKE-LE-ZOUTE

"In the 12 days prior to the show, [Keith] made 200 drawings and paintings and a mural in the casino." **Stedelijk.nl**

Roger Nellens was an interesting man. He was an artist, but more significant for Keith a casino owner, which allowed him to indulge his taste for collecting art. The Casino was renowned for hosting major exhibitions, which in the past had included shows of Picasso, Matisse, Miró, Balthus, Dalí, Tinguely and Magritte. It was Tinguely who suggested to Roger and Monique, his wife, that they show Haring, and so in very civilized fashion they invited Keith to stay with them whilst he put on his show. Keith arrived ready, in his usual fashion, to create his works in situ. He spent many days painting on huge, specially prepared canvases, without any predetermined sketches or plans. In the evenings he would dine with the Nellenses. It was a happy time, away from frenetic New York and the sadness of Andy's death. But then Keith's peace was broken when a reporter from *Newsday* in New York called: "Are the rumours that you have run away to Europe true? Are you suffering from AIDS?"

WHERE?
ROGER NELLENS'S 1960'S CASINO ON THE BEACH AT KNOKKE-LE ZOUTE.

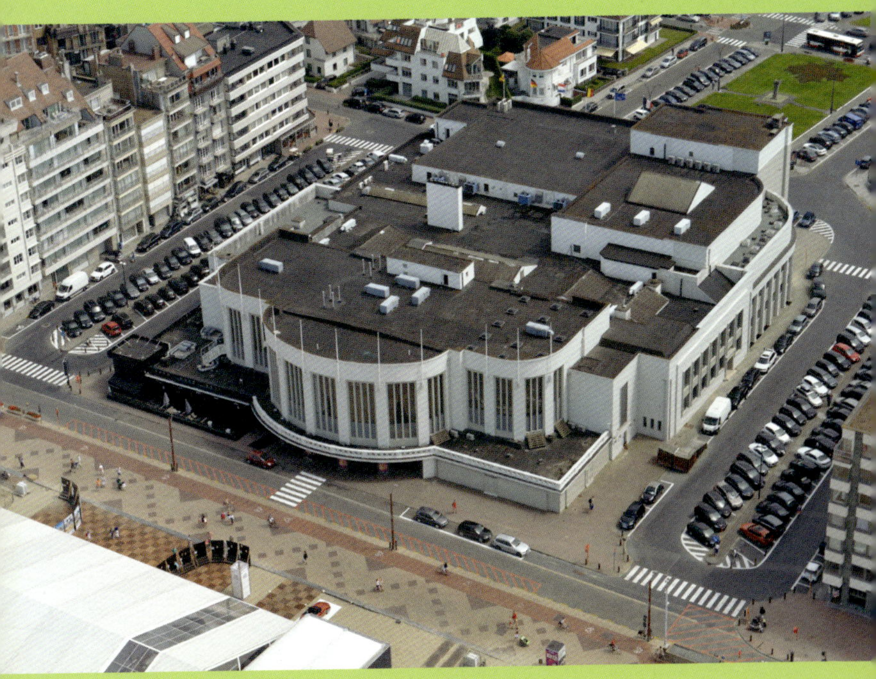

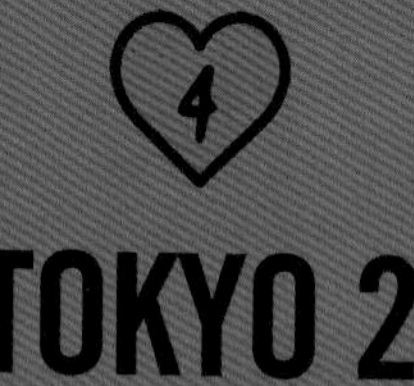

TOKYO 2

"The products were created by Haring to mirror Japan's cultural traditions."
New York Historical Society

The call from New York was like a premonition, but Keith parked it at the back of his head, and headed to Japan to open the Tokyo Pop Shop. Keith had, together with his partners Kaz and Fran Kuzui, come up with the then brilliantly original idea of welding two shipping containers together to create the store. Keith painted every surface of the interiors and packed it with merchandise. Japanese TV and newspapers went crazy for the shop when it opened in January 1988 and there was a big media circus surrounding its launch. Sadly it didn't translate into commercial success. The media frenzy ensured that fake Harings were suddenly available everywhere at far cheaper prices and indistinguishable from the originals. By the end of the year the shop failed and had to close. 1988 also brought depressing news: Keith heard that his ex-lover Jean Dubose had contracted TB, very possibly related to AIDS.

WHERE?
KEITH AT THE OPENING OF THE TOKYO POP SHOP, WITH TWO YOUNG FANS. KEITH WAS GREAT WITH KIDS – AND THEY LOVED HIS ART.

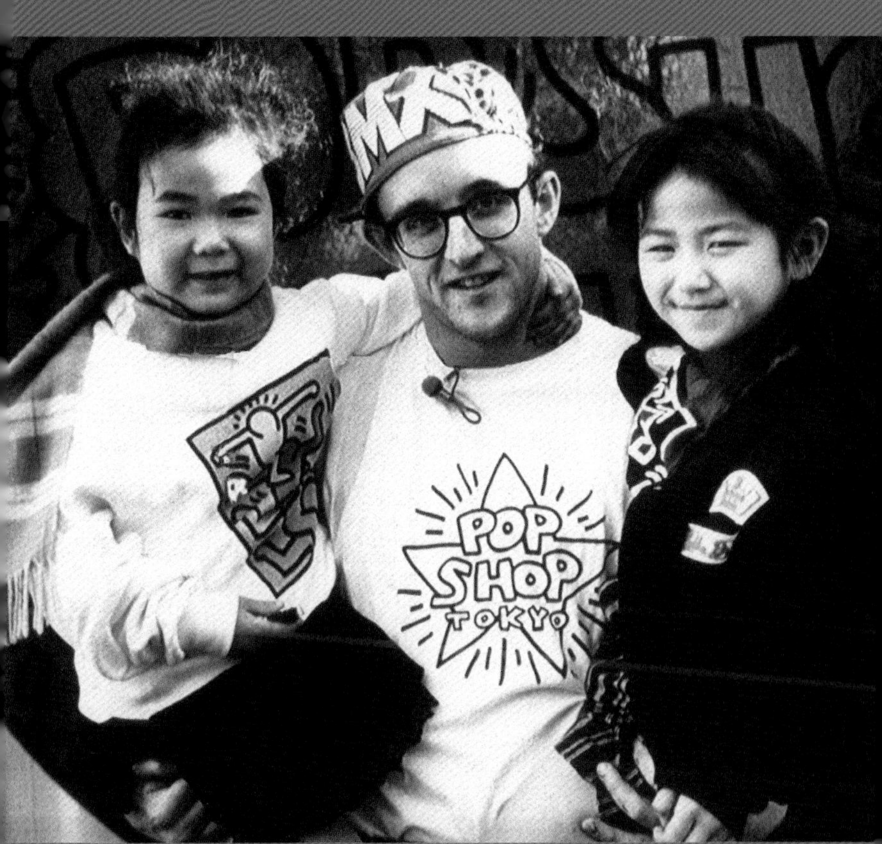
POP
SHOP
TOKYO

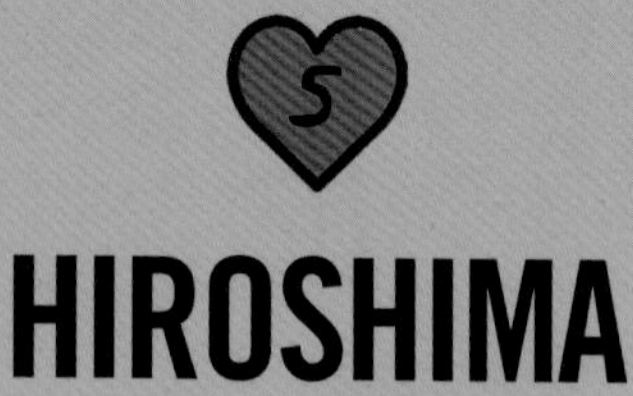

HIROSHIMA

"Peace is a good thing."
Title of the music concert promoted by Keith whilst in Hiroshima.

Keith was in Hiroshima to discuss possibly doing a mural in the city. The news about Jean Dubose was devastating – at the back of his mind Keith knew that, given that Jean had AIDS, it was more likely than not that he might get it too. And there was further news that a number of men who Keith had definitely had sex with, all part of the gay cruising scene in Manhattan, had died. Recent health checks however gave Keith the all-clear and he was optimistic arriving back in Japan. But then, in his hotel room one evening, Keith noticed a tiny purple spot on his leg, a sure sign of the AIDS-related cancer, Kaposi's sarcoma. Keith headed back to New York. Further tests confirmed the worst: Keith was now living with AIDS. Nothing would be the same again. Keith no longer wanted to have sex. He ditched his lover Juan Rivera and took up with an 18-year old, straight, very clever companion, Gilbert Vazquez. Keith now subsumed all his feelings and energy into his love for Gilbert – an entirely platonic relationship.

WHERE?
THE PEACE DOME MEMORIAL,
CENTRAL HIROSHIMA, AT NIGHT.

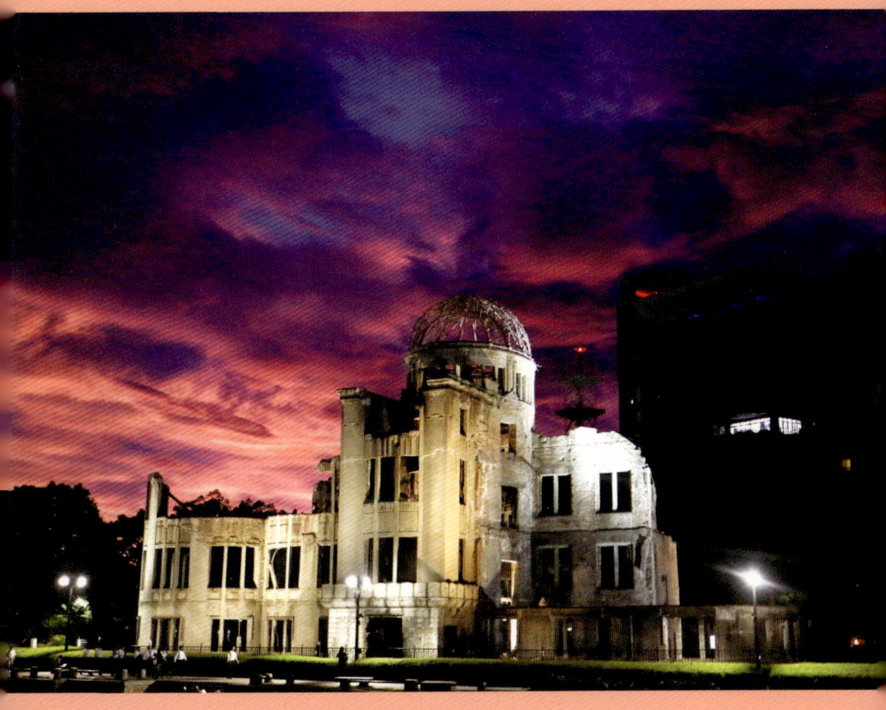

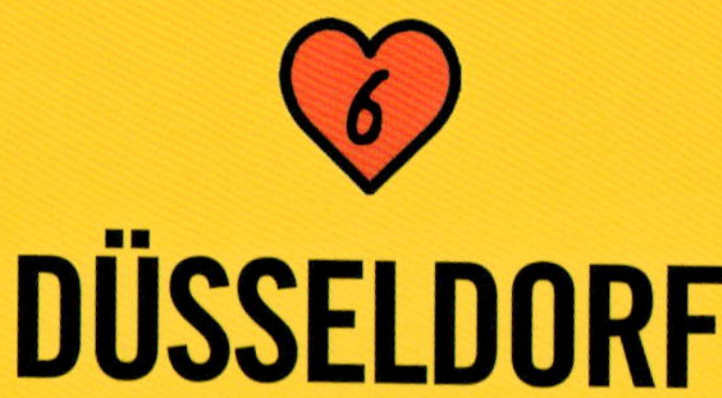

DÜSSELDORF

"Hans Mayer is an art world legend."
artsy.net

Accepting that he had AIDS took a lot of processing. Almost in defiance of what was then almost certainly an early death sentence, Keith threw himself into the production of huge metal sculptures, encouraged by Tony Shafrazi and his German dealer, Hans Mayer. Keith was also acutely aware that the fickle New York art market was moving on from him, turning its attention to the Neo-Geo artists such as Jeff Koons. Germany, Belgium, The Netherlands and France were in effect celebrating Keith's work far more than the USA and, perhaps now thinking he would not be around much longer, Keith also felt disdained by the US museum art establishment. Sculptures were a way around this – a permanent record. The prospect of failure in posterity reared its head. Whilst a show at Shafrazi Gallery later in 1988 was a success and almost everything sold, Haring was smarting that it hadn't been reviewed in either *The New York Times* or *Art Forum*.

WHERE?
NIGHT-TIME VIEW OF DÜSSELDORF, WITH BRIDGE ACROSS THE RHINE AND ICONIC TV TOWER.

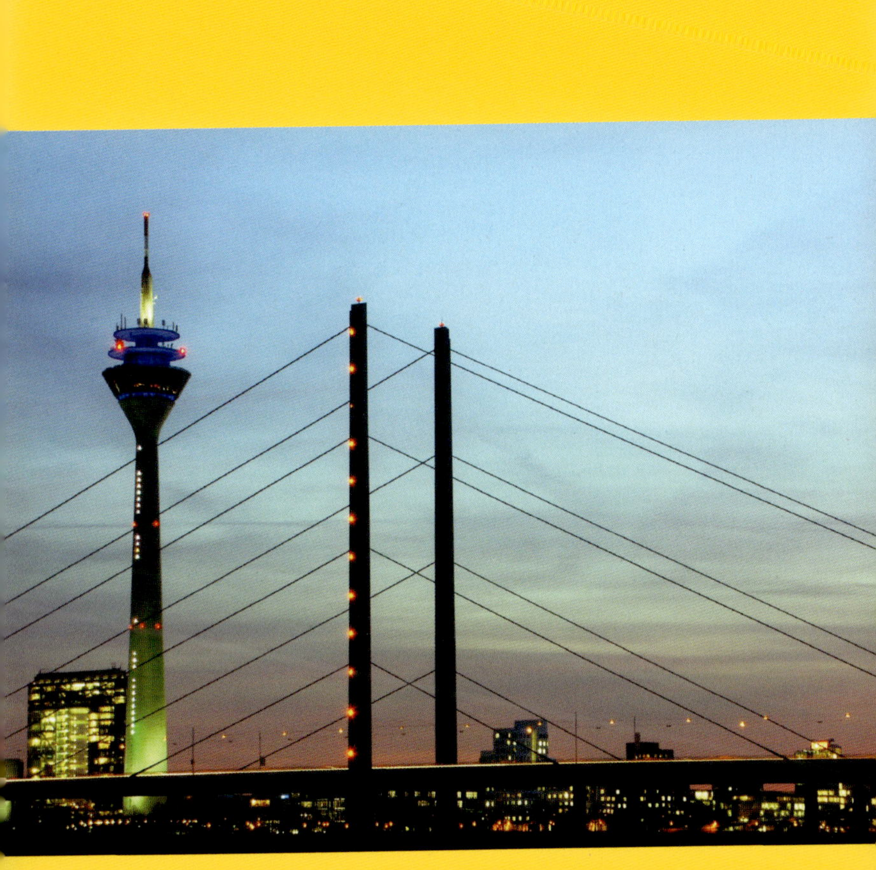

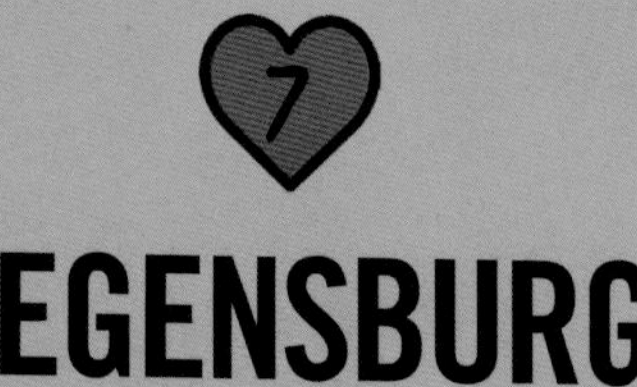

REGENSBURG

"The Punk Princess."

Town and Country, on Princess Gloria 'TNT'.

The death count around Keith was rising. There was Andy in 1987. In 1988 Jean-Michel Basquiat died from an overdose, Bobby Breslau succumbed to AIDS-related complications and then Yves Arman, husband to Keith's good friend Deborah Arman, crashed his Porsche and was killed, driving over from Monaco to see Deborah and Keith in Madrid. To be invited to design her birthday party invitations and decorations by Princess Gloria Von Thurn und Taxis and then attending the party at her Regensburg seat was a wonderful contrast to all the death and destruction. Keith described the party as one of the best of his life, not least for a number of celebrities and guests taking E. For Keith this was a new drug discovery. For a few hours he could completely forget about the HIV virus he was harbouring.

WHERE?
THE VAST THURN UND TAXIS ('TNT') PALACE, REGENSBURG, WHERE KEITH ATTENDED PRINCESS GLORIA'S BIRTHDAY PARTY, ONE OF THE BEST OF HIS LIFE.

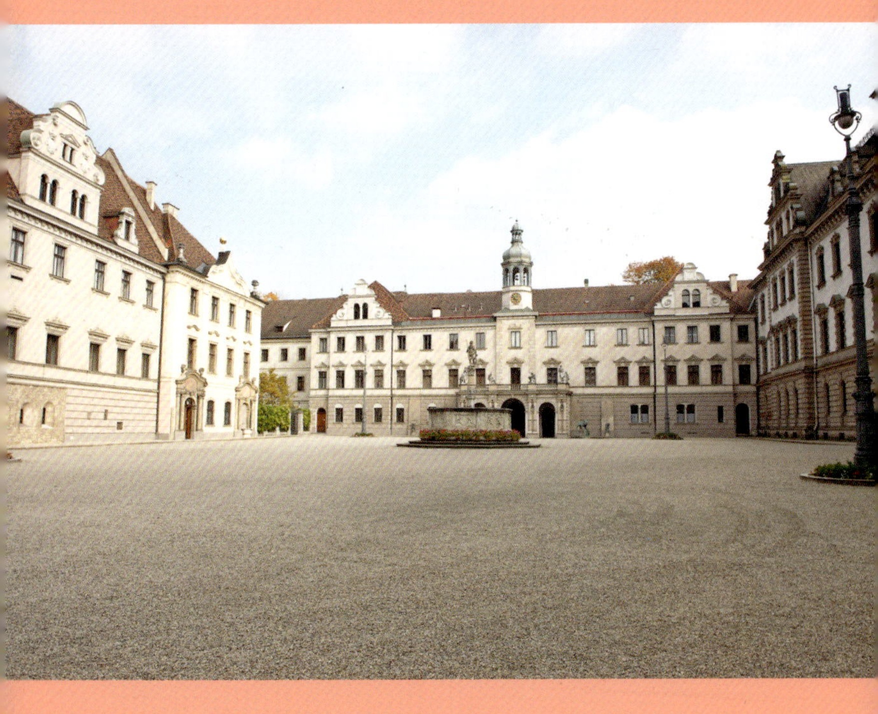

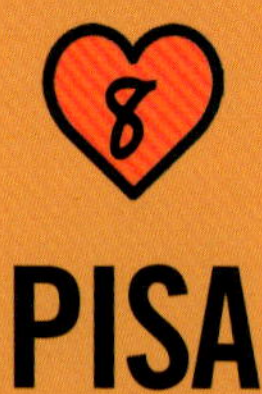

PISA

"This anthem to life only a few months before his death from AIDS."
The Commune of Pisa

It was typical of Keith that a chance meeting on the streets of Manhattan with an Italian and his student son, owners of a vineyard near Pisa, should have resulted in one of Keith's most satisfying commissions: painting a mural on the church of Sant' Antonio in Pisa. Keith worked over a number of days on the 180 square metres of wall, creating an image of peace between men and between man and nature, with the wonderfully medieval theme of Satan, shown as a serpent, being defeated thrown in. The painting, entitled *Tuttomondo*, turned into a big media event, with bigger and bigger crowds travelling from all over Europe to watch Keith paint and getting their Haring T-shirts signed by him. Keith had a wonderful time. He particularly enjoyed his dinners with the friars attached to the church. When the mural was completed the city of Pisa threw a great closing party for Keith, with a sound system and break dancers and skateboarders. Even when facing death, Keith was being utterly life-affirming.

WHERE?
CHIESA DI SANT'ANTONIO ABATE,
VIA RICCARDO ZANDONAI, PISA.

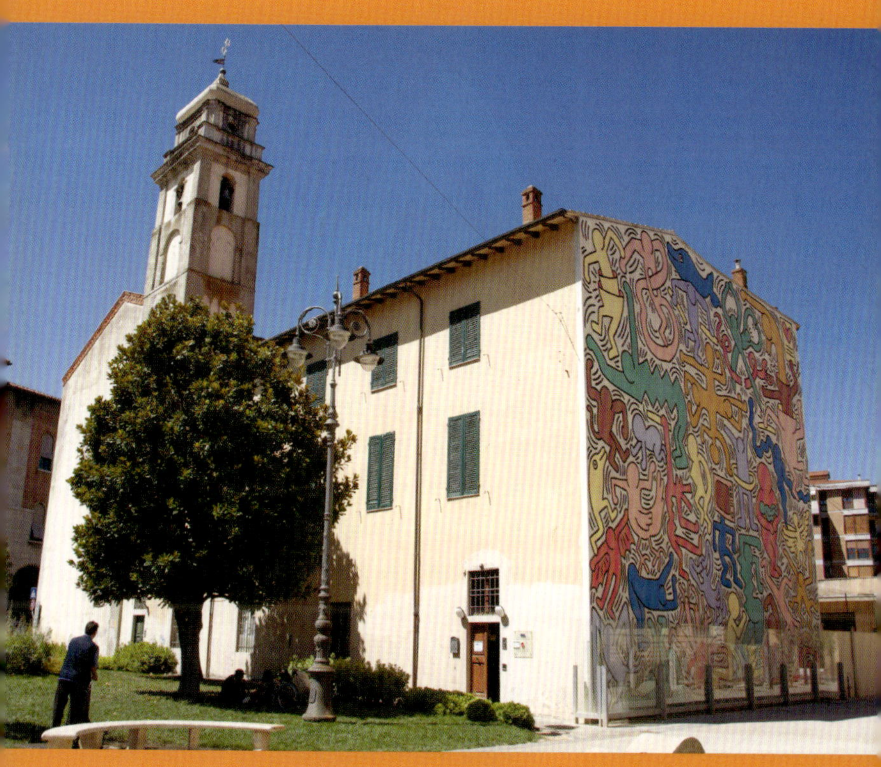

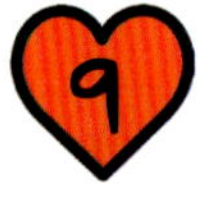

KEITH'S CAMPAIGNS

"The hardest thing is just knowing there's so much more stuff to do."
Keith, Rolling Stone interview, 1989.

Keith's belief that art should be accessible to everyone, his straightforward love of people and in particular babies and children, the inspiration he drew from the street and the way he rejected notions that he was 'selling out' by merchandising his work, meant that using art in the service of activism was a completely natural segway. Even as early as his time at SVA, he had worked activism into his mission, with a manifesto declaring that "The Public Has a Right To Art." It's one of his most enduring legacies, not least in the form of the Keith Haring Foundation. He set this up with great thoughtfulness, after he had had his AIDS diagnosis, in 1989, with the aim of supporting HIV/AIDS research, HIV charities and underprivileged children. It continues its work to this day. In addition to his AIDS work, the list of causes he supported through his art is a long one: Free South Africa; anti-crack campaigns; art campaigns with children; murals for children's hospitals; anti-NYPD racism. Even as late as 1989, Keith was out there, supporting a rain forest benefit.

WHERE?
KEITH WITH MADONNA, SARAH BERNHARD, KENNY SCHARF (ON MADONNA'S LEFT) AND OTHERS AT A DON'T BUNGLE THE JUNGLE RAIN FOREST BENEFIT, BROOKLYN, 1989.

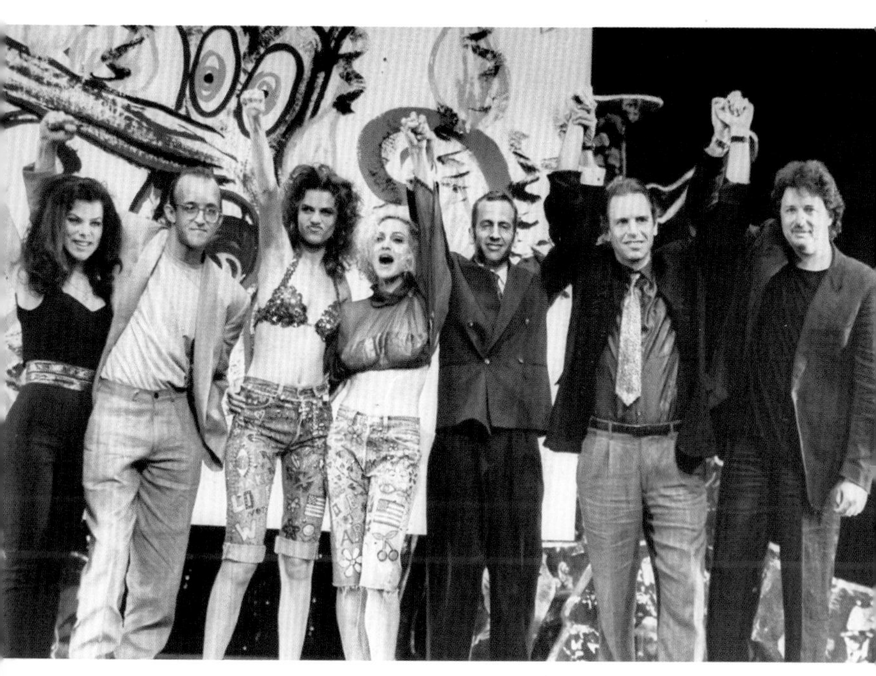

THE SHOCKING TOLL OF AIDS

Like all viral epidemics, it started with a few cases. Initially not even the leading experts knew what they were facing, or how long the possible virus had been incubating for. It could have been decades, it could have been a few years. Not until 1983 was the HIV virus properly identified, and this was also the first year that someone Keith knew had died of AIDS. Soon, however, the numbers started to accelerate, with many leading figures of New York's creative, fashion, music and intellectual communities succumbing to AIDS-related complications. Keith was diagnosed in 1988 and poured much energy thereafter into AIDS awareness campaigns. He died in 1990. By the time the millions poured into research, including from the Keith Haring Foundation, had succesfully found of way of containing the disease, over 400,000 Americans had died as a result of having HIV/AIDS. In 1990, in New York alone, over 5,000 people a year were dying of AIDS. By 1995 this had climbed to nearly 9,000 a year. Below are a few of those individuals, with the year they lost their battle.

Those that Keith knew are in italics.

Klaus Nomi, singer, 1983.
Michel Foucault, philosopher, 1984.
Rock Hudson, actor, 1985.
Ricky Wilson, guitarist, 1985.
Gia Carangi, supermodel, 1986.
Perry Ellis, fashion designer, 1986.
David Summers, actor, 1986.
Liberace, pianist, 1987.
Sam Wagstaff, art patron, 1987.
Bobby Breslau, handbag designer, 1987.
Steve Rubell, nightclub impressario, 1989.
Robert Mapplethorpe, photographer, 1989.
Jean Dubose, DJ and boyfriend to Keith, 1989.
Bruce Chatwin, author, 1989.
Halston, star fashion designer, 1990.
KEITH HARING, ARTIST, 1990.
John Sex, performance artist, 1990.
Kwong Chi Tseng, photographer to Keith Haring, 1990.
Ian Charleson, actor, 1990.
Tom Fogerty, guitarist, 1990.
Freddie Mercury, singer, 1991.
Tony Richardson, film director, 1991.
Brad Davis, actor, 1991.
Larry Levan, DJ at Paradise Garage, 1992.
Tina Chow, model and jewellery designer, 1992.
Anthony Perkins, actor, 1992.
Isaac Asimov, Biochemist and science fiction writer, 1992.
Denholm Elliott, actor, 1992.
Rudolf Nureyev, ballet dancer, 1993.
Cyril Collard, author, 1993.
Arthur Ashe, tennis player, 1993.
Derek Jarman, film director and gardener, 1994.
Leigh Bowery, performance artist, 1995
Eazy-E, rapper, 1995.
Herb Ritts, photographer, 2002.

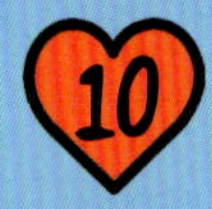

THE RITZ, PARIS

"The Ritz constantly reprimands me for wearing shorts in the hotel lobby."
Keith

Keith liked his luxuries. Straight after Pisa he, together with Gil Vazquez, headed for the Ritz. He loved being the celebrity naughty boy flouting the hotel's dress code, whilst wallowing in its decadent French Empire style. As usual Paris turned into a social whirl, with Keith being invited to the home of the Castelbajacs, hanging out with Sydney Picasso and George Condo, and going to parties hosted by Malcolm McLaren at The Palace. Created in a theatre and formerly the haunt of Grace Jones, Mick Jagger and Warhol, it had become a home to US House and Paris's infatuation with 'Vogeuing' – the camp dance which had originated in Harlem and which was later adopted by Madonna at Paradise Garage. From Paris Keith and Gil flew Concorde back to NYC, before heading out to L.A.. Keith was consciously packing in as much fun as possible whilst he still could.

WHERE?
KEITH AT THE PARIS RITZ, IN 1989.
HE LOVED THE RITZ SO MUCH HE RECREATED THIS BEDROOM IN HIS MANHATTAN HOME.

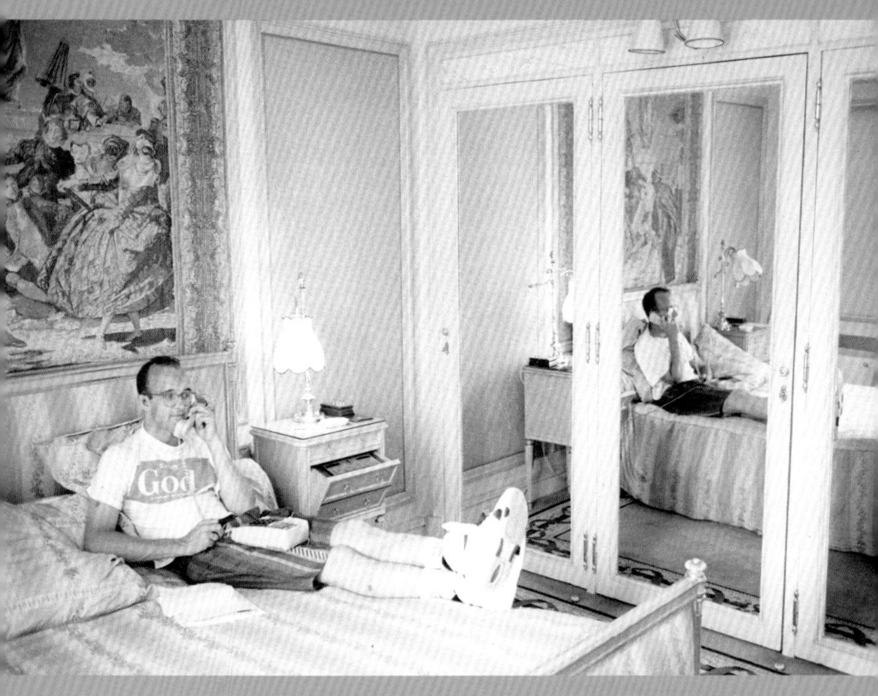
God

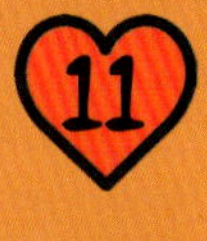

L.A.

"I knew Keith Haring really well."

Dennis Hopper

From New York it was a quick turnaround with Gil to get to L.A.. Right to the last Keith loved, with almost childish enthusiasm, to list the celebrities they hung out with: Madonna, Pee-Wee Herman, Dennis Hopper, Warren Beatty and Ed Ruscha. Martin Blinder, the hugely successful and commercial art dealer in originals and prints of the likes of Chagall, Warhol amd Picasso, had commissioned a big dog sculpture from Keith for his garden, and part of the visit was to watch the unveiling. Keith extracted maximum fun from the visit, including hiring a bright red Jaguar XJS convertible in which he gave Gil driving lessons. 1989 was also however hugely emotional for Keith: he decided to give a completely revealing interview in *Rolling Stone* magazine about his art, his sexuality, his drug use and, of course, his AIDS diagnosis. It was essentially Keith revealing to everyone, not least the folks back in Kutztown, that the party was nearly over.

WHO?

DENNIS HOPPER AT THE FOUR SEASONS IN BEVERLY HILLS, OVERLOOKING DOWNTOWN L.A. IN 1989. HOPPER AND KEITH HAD BECOME GOOD FRIENDS. A FEW MONTH LATER, HOPPER WOULD READ THE EULOGY AT KEITH'S MEMORIAL SERVICE.

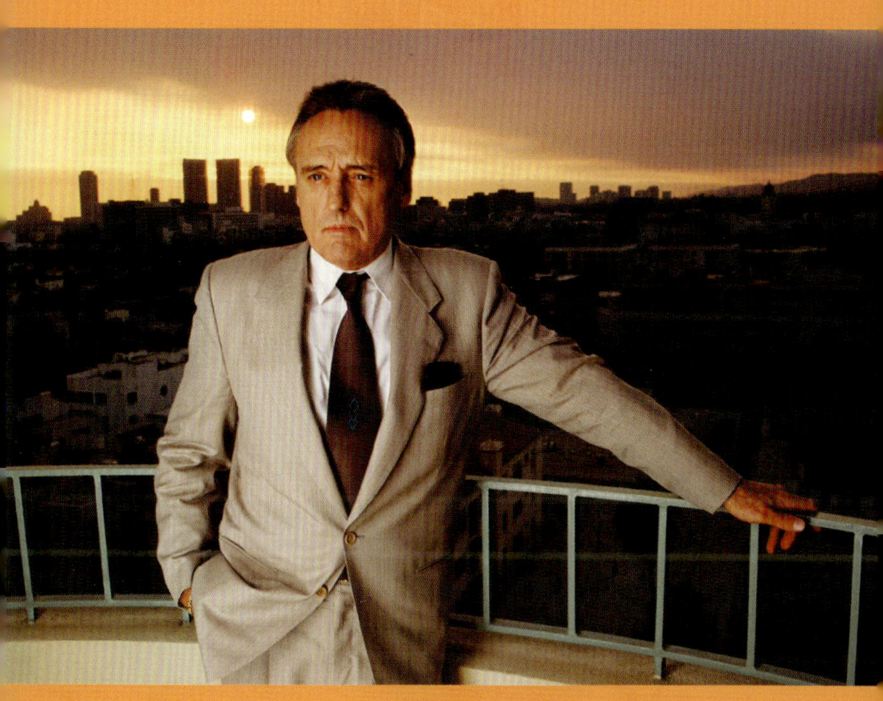

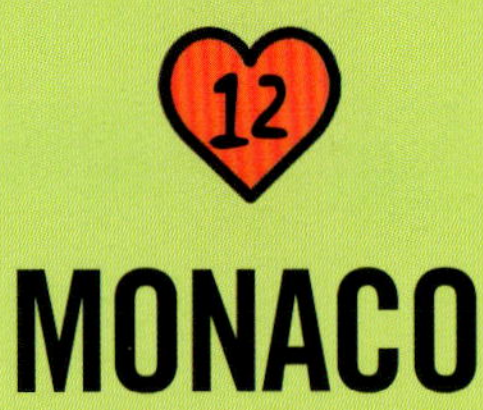

MONACO

Chevalier de l'Ordre du Mérite Culturel

Title awarded to Keith by the Principality of Monaco

When Princess Grace of Monaco, who was a good friend of the Armans, decided to present Keith with the Monegasque Cavalier of the Order of Cultural Merit, Keith decided on a valedictory trip to Europe with his parents. It was their first trip to Europe and their first real insight into the extraordinary life their son had been living. They saw how Keith was feted wherever he went, how the most significant art dealers continued to want to show his work and how, at the drop of a hat, a private jet could be put at his disposal in order that they could all get to the Monaco ceremony on time. Princess Caroline adored Keith and admired the mural he had created as an homage to Yves Arman in the maternity ward of the Princess Grace Hospital, following his death two years earlier. It had been an extraordinary journey from Kutztown Pennsylvania.

WHERE?
KEITH AND CAROLINE OF MONACO AT THE PRINCESS GRACE HOSPITAL, MONACO.

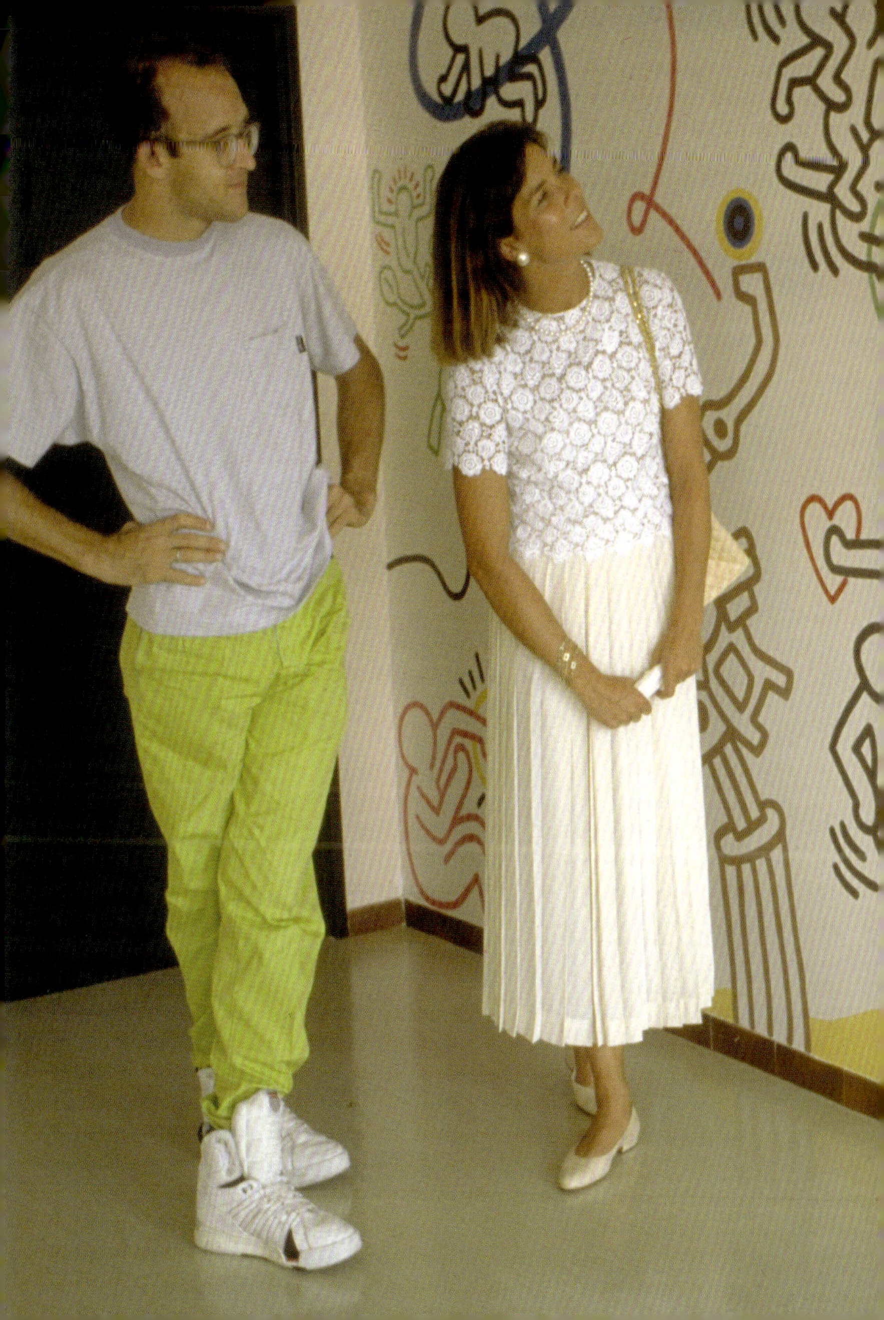

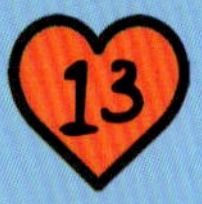

GREENWICH VILLAGE

"Keith Haring created his last drawing, just before his death, for Jean-Charles de Castelbajac." **L'Express, Paris**

Keith headed back from Monaco via Düsseldorf, where he had a commission to paint a convertible for the BMW company. He came back to New York to his new apartment on La Guardia place. Keith had commissioned Yoko Ono's boyfriend, artist and designer Sam Havadtoy, to create the interior and in particular the bedroom, which he wanted to be a copy of his usual room at the Paris Ritz. Keith knew this would be his last home, and his choice of decoration says much about how special his time in Paris had been. He was now getting weaker and weaker, determined to go to his studio to work, but just being unable to. A stream of visitors, realising he was nearing the end, came to pay their respects, as he lay in bed unable to speak. On 16th February, 1990, at 4:40 am, Keith Haring died in his bed, surrounded by the velvet and silk trappings of the French Empire period. He was just 31.

WHERE?
KEITH IN HIS STUDIO IN 1989, STILL WORKING DESPITE AIDS. A FEW WEEKS LATER HE SUCCUMBED TO AN AIDS-RELATED CANCER.

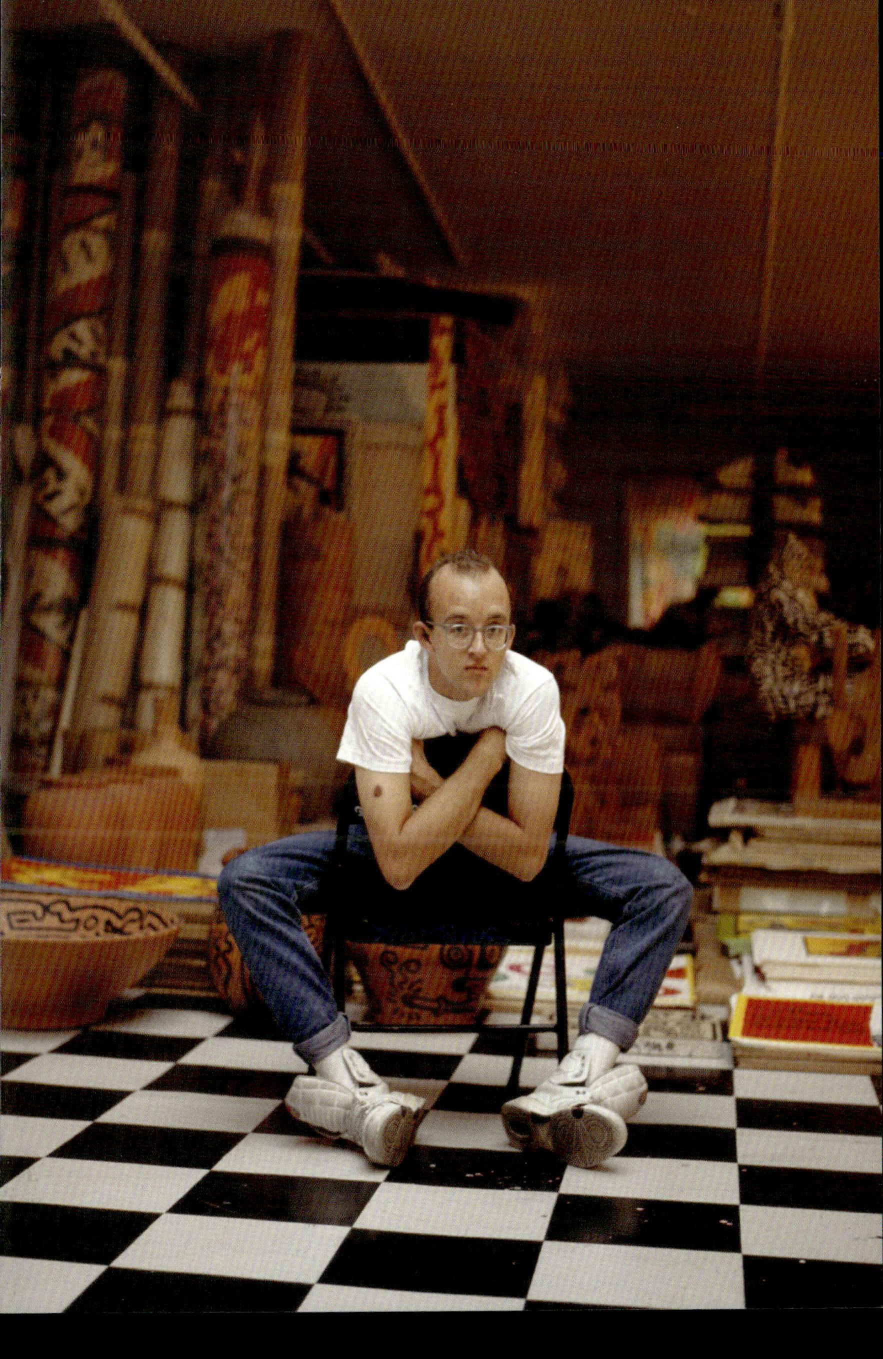

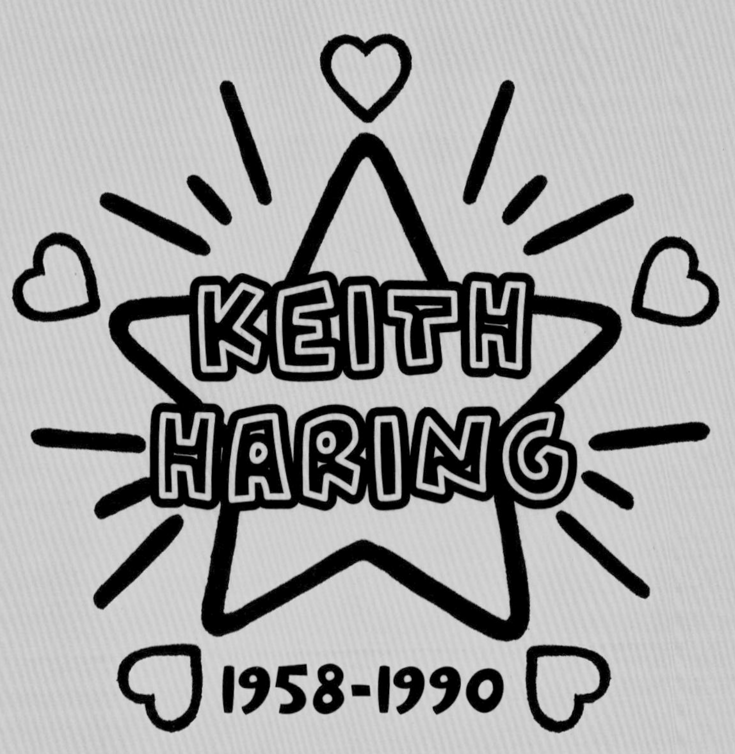

Gilly Lovegrove

CREDITS

Photo credits below are listed in section and page title order. Graffito wishes to thank all individuals and picture libraries who helped track down often elusive images.
In credits below, Alamy = Alamy Stock Photo.

A VERY SQUARE CHILDHOOD
Kutztown PA Alamy
Jesus Saves Alamy
High School Alamy
Long Beach Island, NJ Alamy
The Ivy Art School B. Cendars
Pittsburg Alamy
Carnegie International Alamy

EXPERIMENTING
Christopher Street Alamy
School of Visual Arts Alamy
Rock Lobster Alamy
New York Subway Alamy
CBGB Alamy
Danceteria Alamy
Club 57 Rex Features
SAMO Alamy
Tony Shafrazi Getty Images
The Mudd Club Alamy
The Times Sq Show Alamy

TAKE OFF
The NYC Subway Getty Images
Beyond Words Getty Images
Sixth Avenue Getty Images
Broome Street Alamy
The Dealers Getty Images
Tony Shafrazi 2 Alamy
Documenta 7 Alamy
The Fun Gallery Alamy
Paradise Garage Rex Features
Tokyo Rex Features
Naples Alamy
London Getty Images

SUCCESS IN THE SHADOW OF AIDS
Tony Shafrazi 3 Getty Images
The Factory Getty Images
Grace Jones Alamy
AIDS Alamy
Leo Castelli Gallery Getty Images
The Palladium Rex Features
The Pop Shop Getty Images
Timothy Leary Rex Features
Crack is Wack Alamy
The Berlin Wall Alamy

WORKING IN DEATH'S SHADOW
Andy Warhol Alamy
Paris Getty Images
Knokke-Le-Zoute Getty Images
Tokyo 2 Rex Features
Hiroshima Getty Images
Düsseldorf Getty Images
Regensburg Alamy
Pisa Alamy
Keith's Campaigns Getty Images
The Ritz, Paris Getty Images
L.A. Getty Images
Monaco Getty Images
Greenwich Village Getty Images

Art Director:
Karen Wilks
Managing Editor:
Anthony Bland
Research Editor:
Serena Pethick

Cover and image opposite:
Gilly Lovegrove

A note on the author.
Ian Castello-Cortes is a publisher and writer on 20th Century and contemporary art, with a particular interest in counter-cultures. He is based in London.

First published in the United States of America, November 2020.
Gingko Press Inc.: 2332 Fourth Street, Suite E, Berkeley, CA 94710, USA
Published under license from Graffito Books Ltd.

ISBN 978-1-58423-754-9
Printed in China